Cardigans

Cardigans

Maja Karlsson

Photography Helén Pe

BATSFORD

Contents

Foreword

Is there a cardigan for every occasion? I want to believe there is! Cardigans are like loyal friends: they're there as the seasons shift and the holidays come and go. The everyday cardigan is as important as a cardigan worn for special occasions. Perhaps even more important. It carries us through life – offers warmth when we're cold and embraces us when we need comfort.

Sometimes we need reliability – something to set the compass by. The cardigan can be such a thing. Something consistent in all the fickleness.

I have often worn cardigans when I've been travelling around the world. It is like bringing a little bit of home. I have felt equipped and strengthened. I have also wrapped a cardigan around me when I've been worrying about things both big and small. I've worn cardigans to parties and other occasions. I've been moved and filled with joy – all dressed in a cardigan.

As a knitter you can always create new cardigans for any occasion. It feels promising to cast on when you know that the cardigan will be made for something special. And isn't it a gift to be able to knit your own dream cardigan? Everyday cardigans, special-occasion cardigans, gardening cardigans, travel cardigans, work cardigans, bridal cardigans and Christmas cardigans, the possibilities are endless.

And now a new adventure is about to begin as we explore a year of cardigans, all inspired by the different places we will visit in these pages. In the spring, we'll travel to Stora Skuggan on north Djurgården, the royal game park outside Stockholm, where the wood anemones have begun to emerge and the king's sheep are grazing, just as they have done for hundreds of years. On a warm summer evening, we will go for a slow rowing trip in the archipelago where we will arrive in a small bay at Ljusterö. Here we can marvel at the gorgeous colours of a dahlia garden in full bloom – the flower beds are full of so many beautiful colours. In the autumn we will go out into the forest and to a small fisherman's cottage in Undal, where we can pick mushrooms and gather cones and leaves: a little bit of all the good and beautiful things that the forest has to offer. Then, when winter arrives, we will visit Lilla Hyttnäs in Sundborn and take in the magical atmosphere that Karin and Carl Larsson created together.

I recommend looking at Karin's textiles extra carefully – they never fail to inspire me. Finally, we will celebrate Christmas in Siggebohyttan's miner's estate in Bergslagen which is one of the most beautiful places I know.

I hope you will enjoy this book and that the cardigans you make will be worn and saved – to the very last thread.

Warmest regards from Maja, Arvika, May 2022

About cardigans

The Swedish word for cardigan, *kofta*, comes from Persian's *kaftan*, meaning a long, open robe, and the word can be traced back in Swedish to the 16th century. Sometimes the word *koft* has also been used, such as in epistle no. 63 by Carl Michael Bellman:

> *'... Se där dansar Flickan,*
> *I sin rosenröda Koft and Kiol ...'*
>
> *'... See the girl there,*
> *dancing in her rosy-red blouse and skirt ...'*

I have also encountered the Finnish Swedish expression *buttoned jumper*, and of course the English *cardigan*, which is also used in the Swedish language. Did you know that it was the seventh earl of Cardigan, James Thomas Brudenell (1797–1868), who gave his name to the garment? Around that time the cardigan was a knitted military jacket made from wool, with edges made from fur.

In the Nordic countries, the cardigan has a special place among knitted garments. In Norway, for example, they celebrate cardigan airing day on 15 October every year – a day when those who want can hang their cardigans out to air, so that the neighbourhood can enjoy their gorgeous colours.

And wouldn't it be hard to make it through the year without a cardigan within reach? Convenient, easy to wear and perfect for an evening out whatever the temperature. You can put it on whenever it's needed. It is also perfect for embellishing with different kinds of patterns which is something we like to do in Scandinavia. Our rich pattern traditions have defined our way of knitting cardigans, both aesthetically and practically since cardigans knitted with multiple colours are extra warm, solid and durable. This we can see in places such as Hälsningland, where the colourwork cardigan is included as part of the traditional costume.

In this book subtle cardigans sit side by side with bolder ones. It has been important for me to have it this way, since both versions are needed in life. Therefore, you can find basic cardigans here such as Reed or Silhouette, but also the festive occasion cardigan Dahlia and the Christmas cardigan, Wreath. If you have never knitted a cardigan before you can start with the beginner cardigan, Prima. If you want to celebrate 100 years of women's suffrage, I recommend Sisterhood. Are you thirsty for a challenge? Why not try Legacy – a cardigan that is knitted in the round according to Norwegian principles and then cut open both at the front and at the armholes. Or perhaps you are dreaming of a warming Icelandic cardigan – if so, you should go for Sundborn, the cardigan on the cover of this book. The list is long, and I hope that you will find something that is suitable for you.

In this book are cardigans that are knitted from the top and from the bottom. Many of them are knitted in the round and then cut open. Some are decorated with colourwork sections, others with lace and cables. My hope is that you will discover new techniques and dare to challenge yourself by trying out different methods and constructions. I can particularly recommend the clever button band on the Novel cardigan as well as having a go at adding your own monogram and date to Auntie's Cardigan.

So, without further ado it's time to pick colours, wind the yarn and cast on. My warmest good luck with your cardigan knitting journey!

A few things to keep in mind

- The cardigans in the book are sized according to women's clothes sizes.
- The patterns are divided into three different difficulty levels: 1 = Easy, 2 = Medium, 3 = Advanced.
- To decide which size to knit you need to measure your bust. Then add the ease you would like and compare the measurement with the cardigan's finished measurement. Then choose the size that is closest to your total measurement. Read more about sizes on page 160 in the Knitting School.
- Remember that you can always lengthen/shorten the body and sleeves. If you choose to lengthen, however, you will need more yarn than specified in the description.
- Read the whole pattern first before you start knitting to get an idea of the construction and method.
- For information on abbreviations, see page 163.
- All measurements are approximate.
- The yarn usage specified in the pattern means the number of whole balls/skeins needed, and not the actual usage, which can sometimes be less.
- I recommend knitting a test swatch before you start on the actual cardigan to check that your tension is correct. Make the test swatch approximately 12 × 12 cm/5 × 5 in. Count the number of stitches and rows you get over 10 × 10 cm/4 × 4 in. If your tension is out, change knitting needle size. If you have too few stitches per row for your tension, change to smaller needles. If you have too many stitches per row for your tension: change to larger needles.
- If you can't find the yarn that is listed, you can substitute it with a yarn of the same material and equivalent tension or meterage/yardage.

How to measure the cardigans in the book

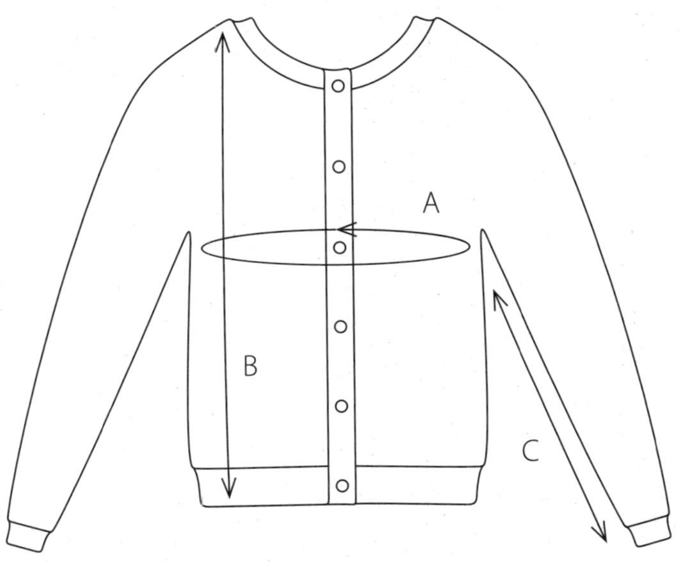

A = Bust
B = Length
C = Sleeve length

Spring is both an end and a beginning. With the milder weather, greenery begins to bud. Everything begins afresh and takes on a new shape.

And it's the same thing every **spring:** at this time of the year I always want to knit cardigans in calm tones. Perhaps my vision for colour comes to life gradually after the winter rest. Eventually I add stronger colours like small islands in bloom among the grey. I start cautiously. One step at a time. As if I were walking along a sun-warmed gravel road and suddenly spotted the first coltsfoot of the year.

When the spring flowers bloom, I take out my yellow glass vase and pick lots of wood anemones. We drink coffee on the veranda, clean out the flower beds and enjoy watching the little lambs that jump around in the pasture. The migrating birds return and everything feels new.

Soon, nature explodes in the most beautiful colours. My heart grows with happiness while my cardigan patterns slowly shift in colour. Welcome dear spring!

Spring Laundry

SPRING

In the past, it was common to gather clothes to be washed in two large laundry sessions per year – spring laundry and autumn laundry. The washing was done outdoors by a stream or the edge of a lake to ensure easy access to water. White laundry made from linen or cotton was boiled in lye in large vats. After boiling, the laundry was taken out and beaten with a washing paddle on a bench or a jetty. To finish, the laundry was rinsed in the stream or lake. Wool was washed in lukewarm water.

The Spring Laundry cardigan is mild in colour, just like early spring. I thought it could be a nice way to make use of leftover bits of wool yarn as you only need a very small amount of yarn for the patterned band. This is knitted at the end of the sleeves and you can choose colours according to taste with favourite yarns from your stash.

Yarn: Svensk Ull 3-ply from Järbo (100% Swedish wool, 100 g = 180 m/196 yd)
Tension: 21 sts × 28 rows in stocking stitch in pattern using 4 mm (US 6) needles = 10 × 10 cm
Sizes: XS (S) M (L) XL (2XL) 3XL (4XL)
Bust: 80 (90) 100 (110) 120 (130) 140 (150) cm/ 31½ (35½) 39¼ (43¼) 47¼ (51¼) 55 (59) in
Length: 52 (52) 52 (53) 54 (55) 55 (56) cm/ 20½ (20½) 20½ (20¾) 21¼ (21¾) 21¾ (22) in
Sleeve length: 45 (45) 45 (46.5) 46.5 (46.5) 46.5 (46.5) cm/17¾ (17¾) 17¾ (18¼) 18¼ (18¼) 18¼ (18¼) in
Amounts: Main Colour 1 = 300 (300) 300 (400) 400 (400) 500 (500) g Gotland Grey (no. 59002)
Colour 2 = 25 (25) 25 (25) 25 (25) 25 (25) g Arctic Fox (no. 59001)
Colour 3 = Small amount of Wasa Crisp (no. 59021)
Colour 4 = Small amount of Helsinge Dark (no. 59020)
Double-pointed needles: 3.5 mm (US 4) and 4 mm (US 6)
Circular needles: 3.5 mm (US 4) and 4 mm (US 6), 60 cm
Notions: 10 buttons (13–15 mm), 8 stitch markers
Difficulty level: 2 of 3
Construction: The cardigan is knitted back and forth on circular needles in one piece, starting from the top and going down – with a patterned band at the end of the sleeves.
Techniques:
SM = slip marker, see Knitting School, page 163.
INCREASES, RIGHT SIDE
M1R = increase 1 st slanting right, see Knitting School, page 163.
M1L = increase 1 st slanting left, see Knitting School, page 163.
CORRESPONDING INCREASES, WRONG SIDE
M1PR = pick up the thread between 2 sts from the back with the left needle and purl through the front loop.
M1PL = pick up the thread between 2 sts from the front with the left needle and purl through the back loop.

Yoke

RIBBED NECKBAND

With 3.5 mm circular needle and colour 1: Cast on 105 (105) 105 (105) 105 (113) 113 (113) sts.

Row 1 (WS): With yarn in front of work, slip 1 st purlwise, *k1, p1*. Repeat from *–* to end of row.

Row 2: (RS): With yarn at back of work, slip 1 st knitwise, *p1, k1*. Repeat from *–* to end of row.

Row 3: As row 1.

Row 4 (buttonhole row): As row 2 to last 4 stitches, yo, k2tog, p1, k1. N.B. Make a new buttonhole the same way every 14 rows, 9 times more.

Row 5: As row 1.

Row 6: As row 2.

Row 7: As row 1. On this row you should also place 4 stitch markers (see Knitting School, page 163): between stitches 22/23 (22/23) 22/23 (22/23) 22/23 (23/24) 23/24 (23/24) = Marker D. Between stitches 34/35 (34/35) 34/35 (34/35) 34/35 (37/38) 37/38 (37/38) = Marker C. Between stitches 71/72 (71/72) 71/72 (71/72) 71/72 (76/77) 76/77 (76/77) = Marker B. Finally, between stitches 83/84 (83/84) 83/84 (83/84) 83/84 (90/91) 90/91 (90/91) = Marker A. The ribbed edge is now finished. Change to 4 mm circular needle and work in stocking stitch back and forth unless otherwise stated.

Row 8 (RS, short row): (Read about short rows and wrap and turn on page 162 in the Knitting School.) Work the first 6 stitches in rib keeping the pattern from the ribbed edge correct. Knit to marker C, SM (see Abbreviations), k6, wrap and turn.

Row 9 (WS, short row): Purl to marker B, SM, p6, wrap and turn.

Row 10 (short row): Knit to marker D, SM, wrap and turn. (Pick up and work wrapped stitch from previous row according to instructions on page 162 in the Knitting School.)

Row 11 (short row): Purl to marker A, SM, wrap and turn. (Pick up and work wrapped stitch from previous row as before.)

Row 12 (short row): Knit to last 6 sts, work the last 6 sts in rib the same way as the ribbed edge.

Row 13: Work the first 6 sts in rib, purl to last 6 sts and work the last 6 sts in rib.

Make raglan increases:

Row 14: Work 6 sts in rib, Knit to last 1 st before marker A, M1R (see Abbreviations), k1, SM, k1, M1L (see Abbreviations), k10, M1R, k1, SM, k1, M1L. Knit to last 1 st before marker C, M1R, k1, SM, k1, M1L, k10, M1R, k1, SM, k1, M1L. Knit to last 6 sts, work the last 6 sts in rib = 8 sts increased = 113 (113) 113 (113) 113 (121) 121 (121) sts.

Row 15 (XS): Work 6 sts in rib, purl to last 6 sts, and work the last 6 sts in rib. **(S–4XL):** Work 6 sts in rib, purl to last 1 st before marker D, M1PR, p1, SM, p1, M1PL. Purl to last 1 st before marker C, M1PR, p1, SM, p1, M1PL. Purl to last 1 st before marker B, M1PR, p1, SM, p1, M1PL. Purl to last 1 st before marker A, M1PR, p1, SM, p1, M1PL, purl to last 6 sts, work the last 6 sts in rib.

Row 16: Work 6 sts in rib, Knit to last 1 st before marker A, M1R, k1, SM, k1, M1L. Knit to last 1 st before marker B, M1R, k1, SM, k1, M1L. Knit to last 1 st before marker C, m1R, k1, SM, k1, m1L. Knit to last 1 st before marker D, M1R, k1, SM, k1, M1L. Knit to last 6 sts, work the last 6 sts in rib = 121 (129) 129 (129) 129 (137) 137 (137) sts.

Row 17 (XS–S): Work 6 sts in rib, purl to last 6 sts, and work the last 6 sts in rib. **(M–4XL):** Work 6 sts in rib, purl to last 1 st before marker D, M1PR, p1, SM, p1, M1PL. Purl to last 1 st before marker C, M1PR, p1, SM, p1, M1PL. Purl to last 1 st before marker B, M1PR, p1, SM, p1, M1PL. Purl to last 1 st before marker A, M1PR, p1, SM, p1, M1PL. Purl to last 6 sts, work 6 sts in rib.

Row 18 (buttonhole row): Work 6 sts in rib, Knit to last 1 st before marker A, M1R, k1, SM, k1, M1L. Knit to last 1 st before marker B, M1R, k1, SM, k1, M1L. Knit to last 1 st before marker C, M1R, k1, SM, k1, M1L. Knit to last 1 st before marker D, M1R, k1, SM, k1, M1L. Knit to last 6 sts, work 6 sts in rib making buttonhole as before.

Row 19 (XS–S): Work 6 sts in rib, purl to last 6 sts, work 6 sts in rib. **(M–4XL):** Work 6 sts in rib, purl to last 1 st before marker D, M1PR, p1, SM, p1, M1PL. Purl to last 1 st before marker C, M1PR, p1, SM, p1, M1PL. Purl to last 1 st before marker B, M1PR, p1, SM, p1, M1PL. Purl to last 1 st before marker A, M1PR, p1, SM, p1, M1PL. Purl to last 6 sts, work 6 sts in rib.

Row 20: As row 18.

Row 21 (XS–M): Work 6 sts in rib, purl to last 6 sts, work 6 sts in rib. **(L–4XL):** Work 6 sts in rib, purl to last 1 st before marker D, M1PR, p1, SM, p1, M1PL. Purl to last 1 st before marker C, M1PR, p1, SM, p1, M1PL. Purl to last 1 st before marker B, M1PR, p1, SM, p1, M1PL. Purl to last 1 st before marker A, M1PR, p1, SM, p1, M1PL. Purl to last 6 sts, work 6 sts in rib.

Row 22: As row 18.

Row 23: As row 21.

Row 24: As row 18.

Row 25 (XS–M): Work 6 sts in rib, purl to last 6 sts, work 6 sts in rib. **(L–4XL):** Work 6 sts in rib, purl to last 1 st before marker D, M1PR, p1, SM, p1, M1PL. Purl to last 1 st before marker C, M1PR, p1, SM, p1, M1PL. Purl to last 1 st before marker B, M1PR, p1, SM, p1, M1PL. Purl to last 1 stitch before marker A, M1PR, p1, SM, p1, M1PL. Purl to last 6 sts, work 6 sts in rib.

Row 26: As row 18.

Row 27 (XS–L): Work 6 sts in rib, purl to last 6 sts, work 6 sts in rib. **(XL–4XL):** Work 6 sts in rib, purl to last 1 st before marker D, M1PR, p1, SM, p1, M1PL. Purl to last 1 stitch before marker C, M1PR, p1, SM, p1, M1PL. Purl to last 1 st before marker B, M1PR, p1, SM, p1, M1PL. Purl to last 1 st before marker A, M1PR, p1, SM, p1, M1PL. Purl to last 6 sts, work 6 sts in rib.

Row 28: As row 18.

Row 29: As row 27.

Row 30: As row 18.

Row 31 (XS–XL): Work 6 sts in rib, purl to last 6 sts, work 6 sts in rib. **(2XL–4XL):** Work 6 sts in rib, purl to last 1 st before marker D, M1PR, p1, SM, p1, M1PL. Purl to last 1 st before marker C, M1PR, p1, SM, p1, M1PL. Purl to last 1 stitch before marker B, M1PR, p1, SM, p1, M1PL. Purl to last 1 stitch before marker A, M1PR, p1, SM, p1, M1PL. Purl to last 6 sts, work 6 sts in rib.

Row 32 (buttonhole row): As row 18.

Row 33 (XS–2XL): Work 6 sts in rib, purl to last 6 sts, work 6 sts in rib. **(3XL–4XL):** Work 6 sts in rib, purl to last 1 st before marker D, M1PR, p1, SM, p1, M1PL. Purl to last 1 st before marker C, M1PR, p1, SM, p1, M1PL. Purl to last 1 st before marker B, M1PR, p1, SM, p1, M1PL. Purl to last 1 st before marker A, M1PR, p1, SM, p1, M1PL. Purl to last 6 sts, work 6 sts in rib.

Row 34: As row 18.

Row 35 (XS–2XL): Work 6 sts in rib, purl to last 6 sts, work 6 sts

in rib. **(3XL–4XL):** Work 6 sts in rib, purl to last 1 st before marker D, m1R, p1, SM, p1, m1L. Purl to last 1 st before marker C, m1R, p1, SM, p1, m1L. Purl to last 1 st before marker B, m1R, p1, SM, p1, m1L. Purl to last 1 st before marker A, m1R, p1, SM, p1, m1L. Purl to last 6 sts, work 6 sts in rib.
Row 36: As row 18.
Row 37 (XS–3XL): Work 6 sts in rib, purl to last 6 sts, work 6 sts in rib. **(4XL):** Work 6 sts in rib, purl to last 1 st before marker D, M1PR, p1, SM, p1, M1PL. Purl to last 1 st before marker C, M1PR, p1, SM, p1, M1PL. Purl to last 1 st before marker B, M1PR, p1, SM, p1, M1PL. Purl to last 1 st before marker A, M1PR, p1, SM, p1, M1PL. Purl to last 6 sts, work 6 sts in rib.
Row 38: As row 18.
Row 39: As row 37.
Row 40: As row 18.
Row 41: Work 6 sts in rib, purl to last 6 sts, work 6 sts in rib.
Row 42: As row 18.
Row 43: As row 41.
Row 44: As row 18.
Row 45: As row 41.
Row 46 (buttonhole row): As row 18.
Row 47: As row 41.
Row 48: As row 18.
Row 49: As row 41.
Row 50: As row 18.
Row 51: As row 41.
Row 52: As row 18.
Row 53: As row 41.

Now the raglan increases for **XL–4XL** are completed. Total number of increases 28 **(XL)**, 29 **(2XL)** 31 **(3XL)** 33 **(4XL)** = 329 sts **(XL)**, 345 sts **(2XL)**, 361 st **(3XL)**, 377 sts **(4XL)**.

Sizes **XS–L** only:
Row 54 (XS–L): As row 18.
Row 55: Work 6 sts in rib, purl to last 6 sts, work 6 sts in rib. Now the raglan increases for **L** are completed. Total number of increases 27 = 321 st.
Row 56 (XS–M): As row 18.
Row 57: Work 6 sts in rib, purl to last 6 sts, work 6 sts in rib.
Row 58: As row 18.
Row 59: Work 6 sts in rib, purl to last 6 sts, work 6 sts in rib. Now the raglan increases for **M** are completed. Total number of increases 26 = 313 sts.
Row 60 (XS–S, buttonhole row): As row 18.
Row 61: Work 6 sts in rib, purl to last 6 sts, work 6 sts in rib. Now the raglan increases for **XS–S** are completed. Total number of increases 24 **(XS)** and 25 **(S)** = 297 sts **(XS)**, 305 sts **(S)**.

All sizes:
Continue to increase for the body by repeating row 1–2 below 1 (4) 7 (10) 13 (14) 15 (16) times. Remember to make buttonholes every 14 rows.
Row 1: Work 6 sts in rib, Knit to last 1 st before marker A, M1R, k1, SM, k to marker B, SM, k1, M1L. Knit to last 1 stitch before marker C, M1R, k1, SM. Knit to marker D, SM, k1, M1L. Knit to last 6 sts, work 6 sts in rib.
Row 2: Work 6 sts in rib, purl to last 6 sts, work 6 sts in rib. Once all increases have been made you should have 301 (321) 341 (361) 381 (401) 421 (441) sts on your needle.

Divide for body and sleeves

Row 1 (RS): Work 46 (50) 54 (58) 62 (66) 69 (72) sts keeping pattern for ribbed edge correct (= right front), remove marker, place next 62 (64) 66 (68) 70 (72) 76 (80) sts on a length of scrap yarn (= right sleeve), remove marker. Knit next 85 (93) 101 (109) 117 (125) 131 (137) (= back), remove marker, place next 62 (64) 66 (68) 70 (72) 76 (80) sts on a length of scrap yarn (= left sleeve), remove marker. Work 46 (50) 54 (58) 62 (66) 69 (72) sts keeping pattern for ribbed edge correct (= left front). Now 177 (193) 209 (225) 241 (257) 269 (281) sts remain on the needle.
Row 2: Work the 6 first sts in rib as before, purl to last 6 sts, work 6 sts in rib as before.

Body

Row 1 (RS): Work 6 sts in rib, Knit to last 6 sts, work 6 sts in rib (slip 1 st at the beginning of each row as before).
Row 2 (WS): Work 6 sts in rib, purl to last 6 sts, work 6 sts in rib.

Repeat rows 1 and 2 until the work measures 21 cm from the division. Finish with a wrong-side row.

Change to 3.5 mm circular needle and make a ribbed hem (k1, p1 and with 1 slip stitch at the beginning of the rows as before), until it measures 5 cm. Finish with a wrong-side row.

Cast off loosely in rib.

Sleeves

Divide 62 (64) 66 (68) 70 (72) 76 (80) sts of one sleeve over 4 mm dpns, as evenly as possible.

Join the yarn by picking up 1 st under the sleeve, k62 (64) 66 (68) 70 (72) 76 (80), pick up another 1 st under the sleeve, place a stitch marker to mark the starting point of the row = 64 (66) 68

(70) 72 (74) 78 (82) sts. Knit 32 (32) 32 (37) 37 (37) 37 (37) rnds. **Dec rnd:** k1, slip 1 st, k1 and pass the slipped stitch over the knitted stitch. Knit to last 3 sts before the marker, k2tog, k1 = 2 sts decreased.

Repeat the dec rnd every 8 rnds another 9 (8) 9 (8) 7 (8) 8 (8) times = 44 (48) 48 (52) 56 (56) 60 (64). Knit until the sleeve measures 35 (35) 35 (36.5) 36.5 (36.5) 36.5 (36.5) cm (or length of your choice). Knit the patterned band following the chart, reading from right to left every row 1–8. (Repeat sts 1–4 until end of rnd, for all rnds.) With colour 2: knit 2 rnds.

Change to 3.5 mm dpns and work the cuff in rib (k1, p1) until it measures 6 cm. Cast off loosely in rib.

Finishing

Weave in loose ends. Block the cardigan carefully according to the instructions in the Knitting School, page 161. Sew on buttons to correspond with the buttonholes.

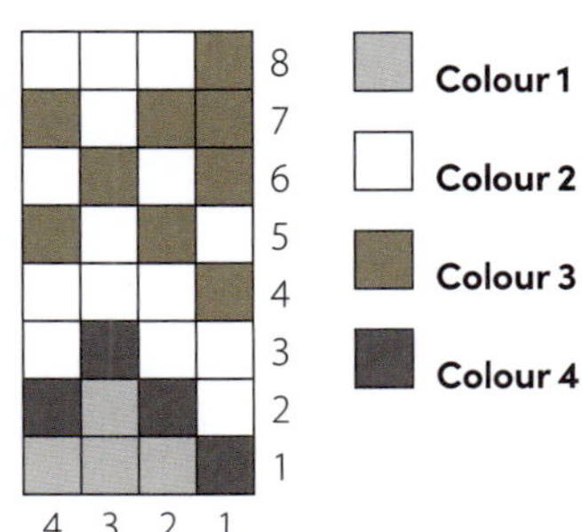

Prima

SPRING

Are you itching to knit your very first cardigan? If so, I want to recommend this pattern!

Prima, which means 'the first', is a soft and comfortable beginner's cardigan, which is also quick to make thanks to the chunky yarn. To make it easier for those who are new to knitting cardigans, I have also added clear instructional images for this pattern.

The construction is seamless, so when you have finished your knitting, you don't have to sew a lot of seams. The cardigan is ready to be worn straight away.

Prima is a good introduction for those who are harbouring a slumbering cardigan knitter within! There are so many fun patterns to discover, you just have to dare to take the first step. Good luck!

Yarn: Børstet Alpakka from Sandnes (96% brushed alpaca, 4% nylon, 50 g = 110 m/120 yd)
Tension: 12 sts × 20 rows in stocking stitch using 8 mm (US 11) needles = 10 × 10 cm
Sizes: XS (S) M (L) XL/2XL (3XL/4XL)
Bust: 100 (116) 132 (146) 160 (176) cm/39¼ (45¾) 52 (57½) 63 (69¼) in
Positive ease: 20–40 cm
Length: 52 (52) 54 (56) 58 (58) cm/20½ (20½) 21¼ (22) 22¾ (22¾) in
Sleeve length: 44 (44) 44 (45) 45 (45) cm/ 17¼ (17¼) 17¼ (17¾) 17¾ (17¾) in
Amounts: 250 (300) 300 (350) 350 (400) g
Cardigan 1: Skotimesønn (no. 8581)
Cardigan 2: Pistasjis (no. 8532)
Circular needles: 7 mm and 8 mm (US 11), 80 cm
Double-pointed needles: 7 mm and 8 mm (US 11)
Notions: Stitch holder
Difficulty level: 1 of 3
Construction: Prima is a seamless cardigan that is knitted from the top down. The upper part of the back is knitted first, then stitches for the front pieces are picked up straight from the back piece. Then the body is knitted together in one piece. To finish, the sleeves are knitted on. The front edges consist of 'raw' rolled edges. Note that the cardigan is oversize. Add 20–40 cm to bust measurement when choosing size.
Techniques: M1R = increase 1 st slanting right, see Knitting School, page 163.
M1L = increase 1 st slanting left, see Knitting School, page 163.
Picking up stitches = see image caption on page 28.

Back

Using 8 mm circular needle: Cast on 61 (71) 81 (89) 97 (107) sts.

Row 1 (WS): Purl.

Row 2 (RS): Knit.

Row 3 (WS): Purl.

Repeat rows 2 and 3 until the work measures 25 (25) 25 (27) 27 (27) cm. N.B. Finish with a wrong-side row.

Place the stitches on a stitch holder/a bit of scrap yarn.

Left front

Now the stitches for the left front are picked up from the existing stitches on the back panel. (See overleaf.)

With 8 mm circular needle: Hold the back panel in front of you with right side facing you. Pick up 23 (28) 33 (37) 41 (46) sts in the 23 (28) 33 (37) 41 (46) sts to the left of the back panel's cast on edge.

Row 1 (WS): Purl.

Row 2 (RS): k1, M1R (see Techniques), knit to end of row.

Repeat rows 1 and 2 until you have 31 (36) 41 (45) 49 (54) sts on the needle.

Then repeat row 1 once more.

Row 3: Knit.

Row 4: Purl.

Repeat rows 3 and 4 till until the front measures 25 (25) 25 (27) 27 (27) cm. N.B. Finish with a wrong-side row.

Place the stitches on a stitch holder.

Right front

Now the stitches for the right front are picked up from the existing stitches on the back panel.

With circular needle 8 mm: Hold the back panel in front of you with right side facing you and start at the right corner. Pick up 23 (28) 33 (37) 41 (46) new stitches in the back panel's cast on edge.

Row 1 (WS): Purl.

Row 2 (RS): Knit until last 1 st on the row, M1L (see Techniques), k1.

Repeat rows 1 and 2 until 31 (36) 41 (45) 49 (54) sts are on the needle.

Then repeat row 1 once more.

Row 3: Knit.

Row 4: Purl.

Repeat rows 3 and 4 until the front measures 25 (25) 25 (27) 27 (27) cm. N.B. Finish with a wrong-side row.

Place the stitches on a stitch holder.

Body

Now it's time to knit the front panels and the back panel together.

With RS of work facing, place all stitches on 8 mm circular needle in the following order: left front = 31 (36) 41 (45) 49 (54) sts, back = 61 (71) 81 (89) 97 (107) sts, right front = 31 (36) 41 (45) 49 (54) sts. Now there is a total of 123 (143) 163 (179) 195 (215) sts on the needle.

Row 1: Knit across all stitches, starting with the left front.

Row 2: Purl.

Repeat rows 1 and 2 until the body measures 23 (23) 25 (25) 27 (27) cm from the armhole. N.B. Finish with a wrong-side row.

Change to 7 mm circular needle and work the hem:

Hem row 1: *k1, p1* and repeat from *–* until last 1 st on the row. Finish with k1.

Hem row 2: *p1, k1* and repeat from *–* until last 1 st on the row. Finish with p1.

Repeat hem rows 1 and 2 once more. N.B. Finish with a wrong-side row.

Cast off loosely in rib.

Sleeves

With 8 mm dpns: Pick up 60 (60) 60 (66) 66 (66) sts starting at the bottom of the armhole opening, up to the shoulder and back down to the bottom of the armhole opening.

Place stitch marker at beg of rnd.

Knit in the round in stocking stitch (= knit all rows when knitting in the round) until the sleeve measures 25 cm.

Decrease rnd: k1, slip 1 st, k1 and pass the slipped stitch over the knitted stitch. Knit to last 3 sts, k2tog, k1 = 2 sts decreased.

Knit one rnd.

Continue decreasing every second rnd until 28 (28) 28 (30) 30 (30) sts remain on the needles.

With 7 mm dpns: Work in the round in rib stitch (k1, p1) 4 rnds.

Cast off loosely in rib.

Make the second sleeve the same way.

Finishing

Weave in loose ends. Block the cardigan carefully according to the instructions in the Knitting School, page 161.

Get started with the Prima cardigan step-by-step

1. Work the first part of the back panel according to the instructions on the previous page.

2. Now it's time to pick up stitches along the left shoulder: insert the needle as pictured.

3. Wrap the yarn around the needle and pick up one stitch.

4. Repeat until you have picked up the right number of stitches. Then knit the left front panel according to the instructions on the previous page.

5. When the left front panel is finished, the stitches for the right front panel are picked up, and are then also knitted back and forth according to the instructions on the previous page.

6. When both parts are done it's time to knit the whole work together so that all parts are worked on the same needle. The body is then finished by working back and forth. Then the stitches for the sleeves are picked up, one sleeve at a time, the same way as the shoulders. Good luck!

Reed

SPRING

Winter and spring are seasons that meet. This is when snow patches and ice floes exist together with catkins and spring sun, all while the reeds sway in the wind. And by the roadside, the wood anemones start to appear. Little traces of life in last year's dry grass. It's a remarkable time. When the year is starting afresh.

The Reed cardigan is a reliable everyday friend. Soft and flexible, it gives just the right amount of warmth for an early spring walk, hunting for signs of new life.

Yarn: Llama Soft from Järbo (85% soft baby llama, 15% polyamide, 50 g = 150 m/164 yd)
Tension: 16 sts × 23 rows in stocking stitch using 5 mm (US 8) needles = 10 × 10 cm
Sizes: EU 34 (36) 38 (40) 42 (44) 46 (48)/UK 6 (8) 10 (12) 14 (16) 18 (20)/US 2 (4) 6 (8) 10 (12) 14 (16)
Bust: 85 (90) 95 (100) 105 (113) 118 (125) cm/33½ (35½) 37½ (39¼) 41¼ (44½) 46½ (49¼) in
Length: 49 (49) 49 (52) 52 (54) 54 (56) cm/ 19¼ (19¼) 19¼ (20½) 20½ (21¼) 21¼ (22) in
Sleeve length: 45 (45) 46 (46) 47 (47) 46 (46) cm/17¾ (17¾) 18 (18) 18½ (18½) 18 (18) in
Amounts: 250 (250) 300 (300) 350 (350) 400 (400) g Soft Sand (no. 58202)
Double-pointed needles: 5 mm (US 8) and 6 mm (US 10)
Circular needles: 5 mm (US 8) and 6 mm (US 10), 80 cm
Notions: 5 buttons (approx. 17 mm in diameter), 4 stitch markers
Difficulty level: 2 of 3
Construction: The cardigan is knitted back and forth, from the bottom up in one piece. Then the stitches for the sleeves are picked up and the sleeve caps are shaped using short rows.
Techniques: M1R = increase 1 st slanting right, see Knitting School, page 163.
M1L = increase 1 st slanting left, see Knitting School, page 163.

Body

With 5 mm circular needle: Cast on 118 (126) 134 (142) 150 (162) 170 (182) sts.

Work the hem back and forth.

Row 1 (WS): p2, *k2, p2*, repeat from *–* to end of row.

Row 2 (RS): k2, *p2, k2*, repeat from *–* to end of row.

Row 3 (WS): p2, *k2, p2*, repeat from *–* to end of row.

Repeat rows 2 and 3 another 2 times.

Change to 6 mm circular needle and work 10 rows in stocking stitch (= knit on the right side and purl on the wrong side). N.B. On the first row, 2 stitch markers are placed to mark each side 'seam' (see Knitting School, page 163), between stitches 30/31 (32/33) 34/35 (36/37) 38/39 (41/42) 43/44 (46/47) and stitches 88/89 (94/95) 100/101 (106/107) 112/113 (121/122) 127/128 (136/137).

Increase row: *Knit to last 1 stitch before marker, M1R (see Techniques), k1, SM, k1, M1L (see Techniques)*. Repeat from *–* once, knit to end of row = 4 new stitches.

Work 9 rows. Make an increase row. Work 11 rows. Make an increase row = 130 (138) 146 (154) 162 (174) 182 (194) sts. Continue in stocking stitch until the work measures 26 (26) 25 (28) 27 (29) 28 (30) cm, finish with a wrong side row.

Cast off for armholes: *Knit to last 2 sts before the first marker. Cast off 4 sts and remove the marker*. Repeat from *–* then knit to end of row = 122 (130) 138 (146) 154 (166) 174 (186) sts.

Now the front panels = 31 (33) 35 (37) 39 (42) 44 (47) sts and the back panel = 60 (64) 68 (72) 76 (82) 86 (92) sts are knitted separately in stocking stitch.

Left front

With 6 mm circular needle: Purl one row.

Decrease 1 st at the armhole. Repeat the decrease on all rows 3 (3) 5 (5) 7 (7) 9 (9) times, then every other row 1 (2) 1 (2) 1 (3) 1 (3) times and fourth row 1 time = 26 (27) 28 (29) 30 (31) 33 (34) sts.

Continue in stocking stitch until the work measures 21 (21) 20 (22) 21 (23) 21 (23) cm from the armhole.

Finish with a right-side row.

SHAPE THE NECK

Following row (WS): Cast off 7 (7) 7 (6) 7 (7) 6 (6) sts at the beginning of the row = 19 (20) 21 (23) 23 (24) 27 (28) sts.

Decrease 1 st at the neck on all rows 5 times, then every other row 1 (1) 1 (2) 2 (2) 3 (3) times and fourth row once = 12 (13) 14 (15) 15 (16) 18 (19) sts.

Work 1 row. Finish with a wrong-side row.

SHAPE THE SHOULDER

(RS) Cast off the following number of stitches at the beginning of every other row 3 times: Size 1: 4, 4, 4 Size 2: (4, 4, 5) Size 3: 5, 5, 4 Size 4: (5, 5, 5) Size 5: 5, 5, 5 Size 6: (5, 5, 6) Size 7: 6, 6, 6 Size 8: (6, 6, 7). Cut the yarn.

Right front

With 6 mm circular needle – re-join the yarn and cast off for armholes starting from the wrong side: Decrease 1 st by the armhole on all rows 3 (3) 5 (5) 7 (7) 9 (9) times, then every other row 1 (2) 1 (2) 1 (3) 1 (3) times and fourth row once = 26 (27) 28 (29) 30 (31) 33 (34) sts.

Continue in stocking stitch until the work measures the same as left front 21 (21) 20 (22) 21 (23) 21 (23) cm from the armhole.

Finish with a wrong-side row.

SHAPE THE NECK

Following row (RS): Cast off 7 (7) 7 (6) 7 (7) 6 (6) sts at the beginning of the row = 19 (20) 21 (23) 23 (24) 27 (28) sts. Then decrease 1 st at the neck on every row 5 times, then every other row 1 (1) 1 (2) 2 (2) 3 (3) times and fourth row once = 12 (13) 14 (15) 15 (16) 18 (19) sts.

Work 1 row. Finish with a RS row.

SHAPE THE SHOULDER

(RS) Cast off the following number of stitches at the beginning of every other row 3 times: Size 1: 4, 4, 4. Size 2: (4, 4, 5). Size 3: 5, 5, 4. Size 4: (5, 5, 5). Size 5: 5, 5, 5. Size 6: (5, 5, 6). Size 7: 6, 6, 6. Size 8: (6, 6, 7) sts.

Back

With 6 mm circular needle 6: Re-join the yarn and cast off for armholes starting from the wrong side.

Decrease 1 st at each end on every row 3 (3) 5 (5) 7 (7) 9 (9) times, every other row 1 (2) 1 (2) 1 (3) 1 (3) times, then fourth row 1 time = 50 (52) 54 (56) 58 (60) 64 (66) sts.

Continue in stocking stitch until the work measures 26 (26) 25 (28) 27 (29) 28 (30) cm. Finish with a wrong-side row.

SHAPE SHOULDERS AND NECK

(RS) Cast off 4 (4) 5 (5) 5 (5) 6 (6) sts at beg next 2 rows = 42 (44) 44 (46) 48 (50) 52 (54) sts.

Next row (RS): Cast off 4 (4) 5 (5) 5 (5) 6 (6) sts, knit until there are 8 (9) 8 (9) 9 (10) 10 (11) sts on the right needle, turn and leave the remaining stitches on hold on the needle for the centre back neck and left shoulder. Work each side separately.

RIGHT NECK AND SHOULDER

(WS) Cast off 4 sts for the neck from the wrong side, work to end of row. Cast off remaining shoulder 4 (5) 4 (5) 5 (6) 6 (7) sts.

Come back to the stitches that were put on hold and cast off the centre 18 (18) 18 (18) 20 (20) 20 (20) sts for the neck, work to end of row.

LEFT NECK AND SHOULDER

Work left side in the same way as the right side but reverse shaping. Cut the yarn.

Sleeves

Sew the shoulder seams using kitchener stitch (see Knitting School, page 164) before knitting the sleeves on. With 6 mm dpns and starting at the centre of the armhole underneath the arm:

With RS of work facing pick up 52 (52) 54 (54) 56 (56) 58 (58) new stitches evenly spaced from bottom of armhole to shoulder, then from shoulder back down to the bottom of the armhole.

Knit short rows to shape the sleeve cap. (Read about short rows and wrap and turn on page 162 in the Knitting School.) N.B. Make sure to pick up and work the wrapped stitches when you pass them. Also the double wrapped stitches that are added when rows 5 and 6 are repeated.

Short row 1: k34, wrap and turn.

Short row 2: p16, wrap and turn.

Short row 3: Knit to the previous turning point, k1, wrap and turn.

Short row 4: Purl to the previous turning point, p1, wrap and turn.

Short row 5: Knit to the previous turning point, wrap and turn. (No increase is made.)

Short row 6: Purl to the previous turning point, wrap and turn. (No increase is made.)

Repeat short rows 5 and 6.

Repeat short rows 3 and 4.
Repeat short rows 5 and 6, a total of 2 times.
Repeat short row 3 and 4.
Repeat short rows 5 and 6, a total of 2 times.
Repeat short row 3 and 4.
Repeat short row 5 and 6, a total of 2 times.
Repeat short row 3 and 4.
Repeat short row 5 and 6.
Repeat short row 3 and 4.
Repeat short row 5 and 6.
Repeat short row 3 and 4, a total of 3 times.
Knit to end of row. Place stitch marker at beg of rnd.
Knit in the round for 8 rnds.

Decrease row: k1, slip 1 st, k1 and pass the slipped stitch over the knitted stitch. Knit to last 3 sts on the row, k2tog, k1.

Continue in stocking stitch and decrease every eighth row until 36 (36) 36 (40) 40 (40) 44 (44) sts.

Cont to knit rnds until the sleeve measures 39 (39) 40 (40) 41 (41) 40 (40) cm.

Change to 5 mm dpns 5 mm and work the cuff in rib (k2, p2) until it measures 6 cm.

Cast off loosely in rib. Make a second sleeve in the same way.

Neckband

With 5 mm circular needle and right side facing: Pick up 78 (78) 78 (78) 82 (82) 86 (86) sts evenly around the neckband.

Work in rib according to the following pattern:

Row 1 (WS): p2, *k2, p2*, repeat from *–* to end of row.
Row 2 (RS): k2, *p2, k2*, repeat from *–* to end of row.

Work another 4 rows in rib.

Cast off loosely in rib from the wrong side.

Button bands

LEFT BUTTON BAND

With 5 mm circular needle and with RS of work facing: Pick up 82 (82) 82 (86) 86 (86) 86 (90) new stitches evenly spaced along the left front edge starting from the top of the neck rib.

Now work in rib stitch:

Row 1 (WS): p2, *k2, p2*, repeat from *–* to end of row.
Row 2 (RS): k2, *p2, k2*, repeat from *–* to end of row

Work another 4 rows in rib.

Cast off in rib from the wrong side.

RIGHT BUTTON BAND

With 5 mm circular needle (RS): Pick up 82 (82) 82 (86) 86 (86) 86 (90) new stitches evenly spaced across the right front edge starting from the bottom.

Work 3 rows in rib stitch as for the left button band, finish with a WS row.

Buttonhole row (RS): Work 4 sts in rib stitch, *k2tog, yo, rib 16 (16) 16 (17) 17 (17) 17 (18) in *. Repeat from *–* another 3 times, finish with k2tog, yo, rib 4 sts.

Work another 2 rows in rib. Cast off in rib from the wrong side.

Finishing

Weave in loose ends. Block the cardigan carefully according to the instructions in the Knitting School, page 161. Sew on buttons level with the buttonholes.

Mirage

SPRING

The Mirage cardigan is designed from memory based on a cardigan that my mum used to wear when I was little. That cardigan was probably the first time I connected with a knitted garment. For me, it symbolizes comfort and safety on many levels, since my grandmother was the one who knitted it.

Mirage comes from French and means 'illusion'. Seeing this cardigan brings me joy since it mirrors an internal image. Like a mirage of the past recreated for the future!

I hope that Mirage is a comforting and comfortable garment to wear for you as well. A cardigan is like a soft armour after all – it protects us from the cold whenever we need it.

Yarn: Järbo 2-ply wool (100% wool, 100 g = 300 m/327 yd)
Tension: 24 sts x 30 rows in stocking stitch in pattern using 3.5 mm (US 4) needles = 10 x 10 cm
Sizes: EU 36 (38) 40 (42) 44 (46) 48//UK 8 (10) 12 (14) 16 (18) 20/US 4 (6) 8 (10) 12 (14) 16
Bust: 88 (93) 98 (105) 110 (115) 120 cm/34¾ (36½) 38½ (41¼) 43¼ (45¼) 47¼ in
Length: 54 (54) 54 (54) 56 (56) 56 cm/21¼ (21¼) 21¼ (21¼) 22 (22) 22 in
Sleeve length: 46 (46) 46 (48) 48 (48) 48 cm/ 18 (18) 18 (19) 19 (19) 19 in
Amounts: Colour 1 = 300 (300) 350 (350) 400 (450) 500 g Emerald Ice (no. 74143)
Colour 2 = 200 (200) 200 (250) 300 (300) 300 g Silver Stream (no. 74104)
Colour 3 = small amount of Tea Rose (no. 74126)
Circular needles: 3 mm (US 2.5) and 3.5 mm (US 4), 80 cm
Double-pointed needles: 3 mm (US 2.5) and 3.5 mm (US 4)
Notions: 11 buttons (15 mm in diameter)
Difficulty level: 3 of 3
Construction: The body is knitted in the round from the bottom up. Then the sleeves are knitted in the round one at a time. Then the parts are joined together on one needle to create a yoke with decreases. To finish, the cardigan is cut open after the button bands are knitted on. Note that the hem and the neckband are knitted back and forth. Also note that the cardigan the model is wearing is knitted in the yarn Tove from Sandnes, which has since unfortunately been discontinued. The substitution yarn from Järbo 2-ply wool, is of the same thickness and quality.
Techniques:
M1L = increase 1 st slanting left, see Knitting School, page 163.
M1R = increase 1 st slanting right, see Knitting School, page 163.

Body

With colour 1 and 3 mm circular needles: Cast on 205 (217) 229 (247) 259 (271) 283 sts.

Knit the hem back and forth:

Row 1 (WS): p1, *k1, p1*, repeat from *–* to end of row.
Row 2 (RS): k1, *p1, k1*, repeat from *–* to end of row.
Row 3 (WS): p1, *k1, p1*, repeat from *–* to end of row.
Repeat rows 2 and 3 until the hem measures 4 cm.

Change to 3.5 mm circular needle and knit all sts. Then cast on 7 steek stitches using the double twisted loop technique (see video links in the Knitting School, page 164). The steek stitches also work as a 'marker' for the beginning and end of a rnd. (Note that the steek stitches don't count towards the cardigan's total stitch count, and any increases or decreases should not be made within these stitches.)

Join into a rnd, taking care not to twist sts. Knit 1 more rnd and then continue in pattern following chart A, rnds 3–19 with the following placement: Repeat sts 1–6 to end of rnd to last 1 st, finish with st 1 in the chart.

Repeat rnds 8–10 with the same placement of the pattern as before until the work measures 26 (26) 26 (26) 26 (26) 26 cm. (Or to length of your choice – if you want you can lengthen the body by repeating rnds 8–19.)

Work the pattern according to chart B, rnds 1–15. Place the pattern according to previous instruction. N.B. On rnd 15, decrease 0 (0) 0 (2) 2 (2) 2 sts = 205 (217) 229 (245) 257 (269) 281 st.

Cast off for armholes using colour 2: Knit 48 (51) 53 (57) 60 (63) 66 sts, cast off 6 (6) 8 (8) 8 (8) 8 sts, knit 97 (103) 107 (115) 121 (127) 133 sts, cast off 6 (6) 8 (8) 8 (8) 8 sts, knit 48 (51) 53 (57) 60 (63) 66 sts = 193 (205) 213 (229) 241 (253) 265 sts. Leave the stitches on hold while knitting the sleeves.

Sleeves

With colour 1 and 3 mm dpns: Cast on 48 (48) 48 (54) 54 (54) 54 sts.

Work in the round in rib stitch (k1, p1) until the work measures 4 cm.

Place stitch marker at beg of rnd.

With 3.5 mm dpns: work the pattern following chart A in stocking stitch (= knit every row when knitting in the round) – repeat rnds 7–18, increase 2 sts every 6 (6) 6 (6) 4 (4) 4 rnds, total 14 (15) 17 (17) 21 (23) 24 times = 76 (78) 82 (88) 96 (100) 102 sts.

N.B. Work the increase rnds as follows: k1, M1L (see Abbreviations), knit to last 1 st on the row, M1R (see Abbreviations), k1. Note that the new stitches should be worked in pattern as it increases at both edges.

Knit until the work measures 39 (39) 39 (41) 41 (41) 41 cm.

Finish after rnd 7 or 13 in the chart.

Work the pattern according to chart B, rnds 1–15 and repeat the 6 stitches to the end of the rnd starting with stitch 5 (1) 5 (5) 1 (5) 1. (The chart isn't easily divisible in sizes, but the transition will be hidden on the inside of the sleeve.)

With colour 2: Cast off the first 3 (3) 4 (4) 4 (4) 4 sts and the last 3 (3) 4 (4) 4 (4) 4 sts = 70 (72) 74 (80) 88 (92) 94 sts. Leave sleeve to one side. Make the second sleeve the same way.

Yoke

Place all stitches from the body and the sleeves on a 3.5 mm circular needle, with the sleeves positioned over the cast off

stitches on the body = 333 (349) 361 (389) 417 (437) 453 sts.
With colour 2, sizes 36, 38, 42, 44, 46 and 48: Work in stocking stitch and decrease 2 (1) 7 (1) 4 (3) evenly spaced across the first rnd = 331 (348) – (382) – (416) (433) (450) sts.

Size 40: Work in stocking stitch and increase 4 sts evenly spaced across the first rnd = 365 sts.

331 (348) 365 (382) 416 (433) 450 sts.

All sizes: Knit another 6 rows.

Dec rnd 1: k7, *k15, k2tog*. Repeat from *–* to last 1 st (apart from the steek stitches), k1 = 312 (328) 344 (360) 392 (408) 424 sts. Knit 5 (5) 5 (6) 6 (6) 6 rnds.

Dec rnd 1: k7 *k14, k2tog*. Repeat from *–* to last 1 st (apart from the steek stitches), k1 = 293 (308) 323 (338) 368 (383) 398 sts. Knit 5 (5) 5 (6) 6 (6) 6 rnds.

Dec rnd 3: k7, *k13, k2tog*. Repeat from *–* to last 1 st (apart from the steek stitches), k1 = 274 (288) 302 (316) 344 (358) 372 sts. Knit 3 (3) 3 (3) 3 (6) 6 rnds.

Dec rnd 4: k7, *k12, k2tog*. Repeat from *–* to last 1 st (apart from the steek stitches), k1 = 255 (268) 281 (294) 320 (333) 346 sts. Knit 3 (3) 3 (3) 3 (3) 6 rnds.

Dec rnd 5: k7, *k11, k2tog*. Repeat from *–* to last 1 st (apart from the steek stitches), k1 = 236 (248) 260 (272) 296 (308) 320 sts. Knit 3 rnds.

Dec rnd 6: k7, *k10, k2tog*. Repeat from *–* to last 1 st (apart from the steek stitches), k1 = 217 (228) 239 (250) 272 (283) 294 sts. Knit 3 rnds.

Dec rnd 7: k7, *k9, k2tog*. Repeat from *–* to last 1 st (apart from the steek stitches), k1 = 198 (208) 218 (228) 248 (258) 268 sts. Knit 3 rnds.

Dec rnd 8: k7, *k8, k2tog*. Repeat from *–* to last 1 st (apart from the steek stitches), k1 = 179 (188) 197 (206) 224 (233) 242 sts. Knit 17 rnds.

Dec rnd 9: k7, *k7, k2tog*. Repeat from *–* to last 1 st (apart from the steek stitches), k1 = 160 (168) 176 (184) 200 (208) 216 sts. Knit 3 rnds.

Dec rnd 10: *k6, k2tog*. Repeat from *–* = 140 (147) 154 (161) 175 (182) 199 sts. Knit 1 rnd.

Dec rnd 11: Knit and decrease 7 (14) 17 (22) 32 (35) 52 sts evenly spaced across the rnd = 133 (133) 137 (139) 143 (147) 147 sts.

Cast off the 7 steek stitches at the end of the rnd.

Change to 3 mm circular needle and work in rib back and forth:

Row 1 (RS): k1, *p1, k1*, repeat from *–* to end of row.

Row 2 (WS): p1, *k1, p1*, repeat from *–* to end of row.

Repeat rows 1 and 2 until you have worked a total of 6 rows in rib. Cast off loosely in rib.

Button bands

LEFT BUTTON BAND

With 3 mm circular needle and colour 2 (RS): Pick up stitches along the left front edge starting from the top. To make sure the edge is flexible, pick up 3 out of 4 sts (each stitch relates to a row of the Front) (e.g. *k3 sts, skip the 4th st*, repeat from *–*). Make sure you have an odd number of stitches.

Work in rib stitch:

Row 1 (WS): *p1, k1*, repeat from *–* to last st, p1.

Row 2 (RS): *k1, p1*, repeat from *–* to last st, k1.

Row 3 (WS): *p1, k1*, repeat from *–* to last st, p1.

Repeat rows 2 and 3 a total of 5 times = 11 rows.

Cast off in rib stitch.

RIGHT BUTTON BAND

With 3 mm circular needle and colour 2, from the right side: Pick up stitches along the right front edge starting from the bottom. Make sure to pick up the same number of stitches as on the left side. Place markers on needle for 11 buttonholes spaced evenly along the edge (each buttonhole goes over 2 sts).

Work in rib stitch according to the instructions for the left side up to and including row 5.

Row 6 (buttonhole row 1, RS): Work in rib until you get to the first buttonhole. Then as follows:

yo, k2tog, continue in established rib until you get to the next buttonhole. Repeat from *–* until all buttonholes have been finished and then work in rib to end of row.

Row 7 (buttonhole row 2, WS): Work in rib as set to end of row.

Work another 4 rows in rib and then cast off in rib.

Cutting the steek

See Knitting School, page 160. Sew a reinforcing seam with sewing thread (by hand using backstitch) on each side of the middle steek stitch. Carefully cut the cardigan open in the middle of the middle steek stitch. (The cut edges will roll in towards the wrong side.) Either cover the cut edges on the inside with a decorative band, or fold them in and sew with discreet stitches to the wrong side (see Knitting School, pages 160-161).

Chart A

Chart B

Colour 1

Colour 2

Colour 3

Finishing

Sew the underarm holes together using kitchener stitch (see Knitting School, page 164). Weave in loose ends. Block the cardigan carefully according to the instructions in the Knitting School, page 161. Sew in buttons in height with the buttonholes.

A couple of years ago, hundreds of butterflies gathered in a thicket in our neighbouring village. It was a magical sight. None of us knew why – you never know with butterflies – but I was pleased that they were there. The next **summer** I went for a walk in the forest by the cabin. Suddenly I spotted something that I had never seen before – a flowering spruce, completely covered in little red cones at the top. Nature never stops serving up surprises and that's why I love to be as close to it as possible.

So I sit down on the old stone steps with my knitting in my hands and watch out over the landscape. In the garden the peonies are flowering, and the garden birds are circling over the slate roof. The hops are climbing and the sheep are bleating. The air is warm and a herding dog comes to say hello.

It's during these weeks that we go for walks. I absorb all the colours and shapes of the forest, thinking that I will memorize these for knitting later in the autumn. But for now, it's summer when I love taking an evening dip. On the way home I wrap my softest cardigan around me.

Midsummer

Midsummer's Eve is characterized by flowers, leaf-decorated wagons, circle dance, accordions and partying. Rain sometimes too, of course, but those who celebrate midsummer are used to it! After all, it's not about the weather, it's about friends, family, tradition and having a good time. Lasting memories are created, like when my daughter Greta and I got a lift on our neighbour's tractor to the summer festivities. Or all the summers with friends when we danced well into the evening. I remember as a child when I dressed in a homemade folk costume at the park in Balders Hage. So many precious moments of Swedish summers gone by.

Then midsummer evening always comes. A veil of mist covers the pastures and soon that particular magic of midsummer's night arrives. Perhaps this is when you need a cardigan to wrap around your shoulders...

Yarn: Rauma Finull from Rauma Ullvarefabrikk (100% pure new wool, 50 g = 175 m/191 yd)
Tension: 24 sts × 30 rows in stocking stitch in pattern using 3 mm (US 2.5) needles = 10 × 10 cm
Sizes: S/M (L/XL) 2XL
Bust: 90 (108) 124 cm/35½ (42½) 48¾ in
Length: 50 (52) 54 cm/19¾ (20½) 21¼ in
Sleeve length: 52 (53) 54 cm/20½ (20¾) 21¼ in
Amounts: Colour 1 = 300 (350) 400 g Lyng (no. 427)
Colour 2 = 50 (50) 50 g Natur (no. 401)
Colour 3 = 50 (50) 50 g Jadegrønn (no. 4215)
Colour 4 = 25 (25) 25 g Gammelrosa (no. 4571)
Double-pointed needles: 2.5 mm (US 1.5) and 3 mm (US 2.5)
Circular needles: 2.5 mm (US 1.5) and 3 mm (US 2.5), 80 cm
Notions: 9 buttons (15 mm in diameter), 13–17 stitch markers, stitch holder, decorative band (optional)
Difficulty level: 3 of 3
Construction: The cardigan is knitted in the round from the top down – yoke, body and then sleeves. Then the cardigan is cut open at the front (see Knitting School, page 160), after the button bands and neckband are knitted on.
Techniques: Short rows and wrap and turn = see Knitting School, page 162.
M1R = increase 1 st slanting right, see Knitting School, page 163.
M1b = increase 1 st in the stich below, see Knitting School, page 163.
M1L = increase 1 st slanting left, see Knitting School, page 163.

Yoke

With 3 mm circular needle and colour 1: Cast on 138 (148) 154 sts (5 of these stitches make out the steek where the finished cardigan is cut open).

Now work according to the charts given. Follow the rows of each chart starting on the row according to the size you are making for every chart – A, B/C, D, E & F.

Sizes **S/M** rows 5–37, Sizes **L/XL** rows (3–37), Size **2XL** rows 1–37 with the following placement:

Work each chart as follows: Knit 3 (steek), chart A, chart B/C 5 (6) 7 times, chart D, chart E 4 (5) 6 times and then work chart F, k2 (= steek). At the same time, make the increases as specified in the charts = 330 (386) 442 sts.

Work in stocking stitch rnds (= knit all rows when knitting in the round).

Knit the colourwork pattern according to chart G with the following placement, rnds 1–25:

S/M: k3 (= steek), work stitches 7–8, then repeat stitches 1–8 in the chart to last 5 sts, work stitches 1–3, k2 (= steek).

L/XL: k3 (= steek), work stitches 7–8, then repeat stitches 1–8 in the chart to last 5 sts, work stitches 1–3, k2 (= steek).

2XL: k3 (= steek), repeat stitches 1–8 in the chart to last 3 sts, work stitch 1, k2 (= steek).

With colour 1: Knit another 2 (8) 10 rnds.

Body

K3 (= steek), k48 (57) 68 sts (= left front) and place next 68 (78) 84 sts on a stitch holder/scrap yarn (= left sleeve stitches).

Cast on 6 new stitches, place a stitch marker (= centre-underarm) and cast on 6 new stitches.

Knit 93 (111) 133 sts (= back) and place next 68 (78) 84 sts on a stitch holder (= right sleeve stitches).

Cast on 6 new stitches, place a stitch marker (= centre-underarm) and cast on 6 new stitches.

Knit 48 (57) 68 sts, k2 (= steek) (= right front) = total 218 (254) 298 sts.

Knit until the work measures 24 (25) 26 cm. Cast off the 5 steek stitches on the last rnd.

Change to 2.5 mm circular needle and work in rib stitch (k1, p1) back and forth to last 1 st on the row, finish with k1. When the rib measures 4 cm: Cast off loosely in rib.

Sleeves

With 3 mm dpns and colour 1: Pick up 6 sts starting from the marker at the underarm (where you cast on new stitches for the body before). Knit the 68 (78) 84 sts from the stitch holder, pick up another 6 sts under the sleeve = 80 (90) 96 sts. Knit until the sleeve measures 7 (5) 5 cm.

Dec rnd: k1, slip 1 st, k1 and pass the slipped stitch over the knitted stitch. Knit to last 3 sts before the marker, k2tog, k1 = 2 sts decreased.

Repeat the decrease rows every 3.5 (3) 3 cm, a total of 12 (15) 15 times. Now 24 sts have been decreased = 56 (60) 66 sts.

Knit until the sleeve measures 48 cm.

Change to 2.5 mm dpns and work in rib (k1, p1) for 4 cm. Cast off loosely in rib.

Make second sleeve the same way.

Button bands

LEFT FRONT EDGE

With 2.5 mm circular needle, colour 1 and right side facing: Pick up 113 (117) 121 sts along the left front edge starting from the top.

Now work in rib stitch:

Row 1 (WS): *p1, k1*. Repeat from *–* to last 1 st, p1.

Row 2 (RS): *k1, p1*. Repeat from *–* to last 1 st, k1.

Repeat rows 1 and 2, a total of 6 times (= 12 rows in total). Cast off loosely in rib from the wrong side.

RIGHT FRONT EDGE

With 2.5 mm circular needle, colour 1 and with right side facing: Pick up 113 (117) 121 st along the right front edge starting from the bottom.

Work in rib according to the description for the left button band up to and including row 55:

Row 6 (buttonhole row 1, RS): Work 4 (6) 4 sts in rib, *cast off 2 sts, work 11 (11) 12 sts in rib*. Repeat from *–* 7 times more, cast off 2 sts, work 3 (5) 3 sts in rib.

Row 7 (buttonhole row 2, WS): Work 3 (5) 3 sts in rib, cast on 2 new sts, * work 11 (11) 12 sts in rib, cast on 2 new stitches*. Repeat from *–* 7 times, work 4 (6) 4 sts in rib. Work another 5 rows in rib. Cast off in rib from the wrong side.

Neckband

With 2.5 mm circular needle and colour 1: Pick up 131 (153) 175 sts evenly spaced around the neckband.

Knit 37 (43) 49 and place a stitch marker that now marks the start of the row. (Read about short rows and wrap and turn on page 162 in the Knitting School.)

Short row 1: Knit 57 (67) 77, wrap and turn.

Short row 2: Knit 62 (72) 82, wrap and turn.

Short row 3: Knit 67 (77) 87, wrap and turn.

Short row 4: Knit 72 (82) 92, wrap and turn.

Short row 5: Knit 77 (87) 97, wrap and turn.

Short row 6: Knit back over all sts until you reach the centre of the front.

Knit a whole row – at the same time, decrease 8 (10) 12 sts evenly spaced across the row = 123 (143) 163 sts.

Knit 5 rows in garter st. Cast off.

Cutting the steek

See Knitting School, page 160. Sew a reinforcing seam with sewing thread (by hand using backstitch) on each side of the middle steek stitch. Carefully cut the cardigan open in the middle of the middle steek stitch. (The cut edges will roll in towards the wrong side.)

Finishing

Weave in loose ends. Block the cardigan carefully according to the instructions in the Knitting School, page 161. Sew in buttons in height with the buttonholes. Either cover the cut edges on the inside with a decorative band, or fold them in and sew with discreet stitches to the wrong side (see Knitting School, pages 160–161).

Chart A

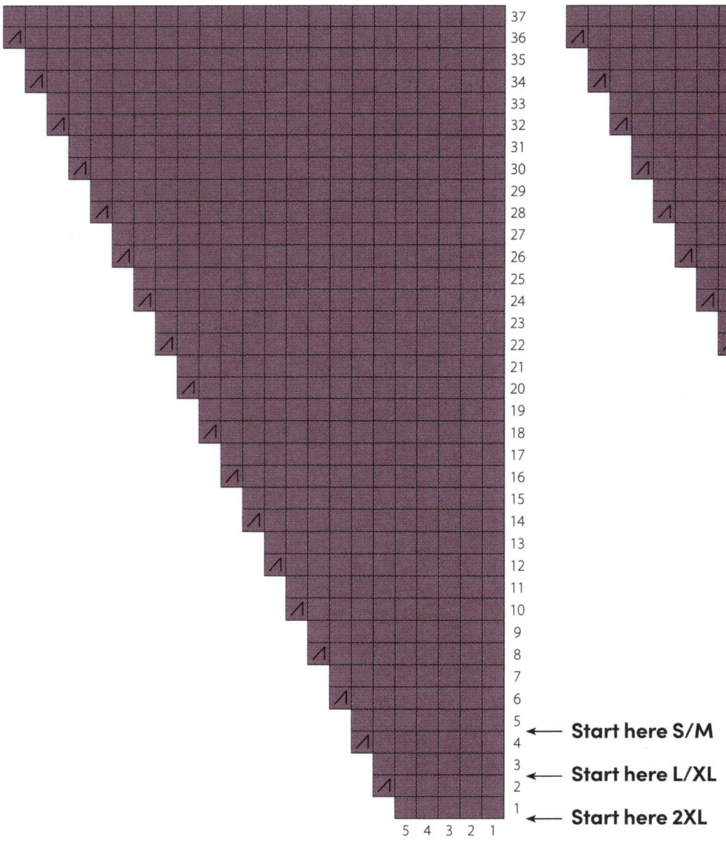

37
36
35
34
33
32
31
30
29
28
27
26
25
24
23
22
21
20
19
18
17
16
15
14
13
12
11
10
9
8
7
6
5 ← **Start here S/M**
4
3 ← **Start here L/XL**
2
1 ← **Start here 2XL**

5 4 3 2 1

Chart B/C

37
36
35
34
33
32
31
30
29
28
27
26
25
24
23
22
21
20
19
18
17
16
15
14
13
12
11
10
9
8
7
6
5 ← **Start here S/M**
4
3 ← **Start here L/XL**
2
1 ← **Start here 2XL**

10 9 8 7 6 5 4 3 2 1

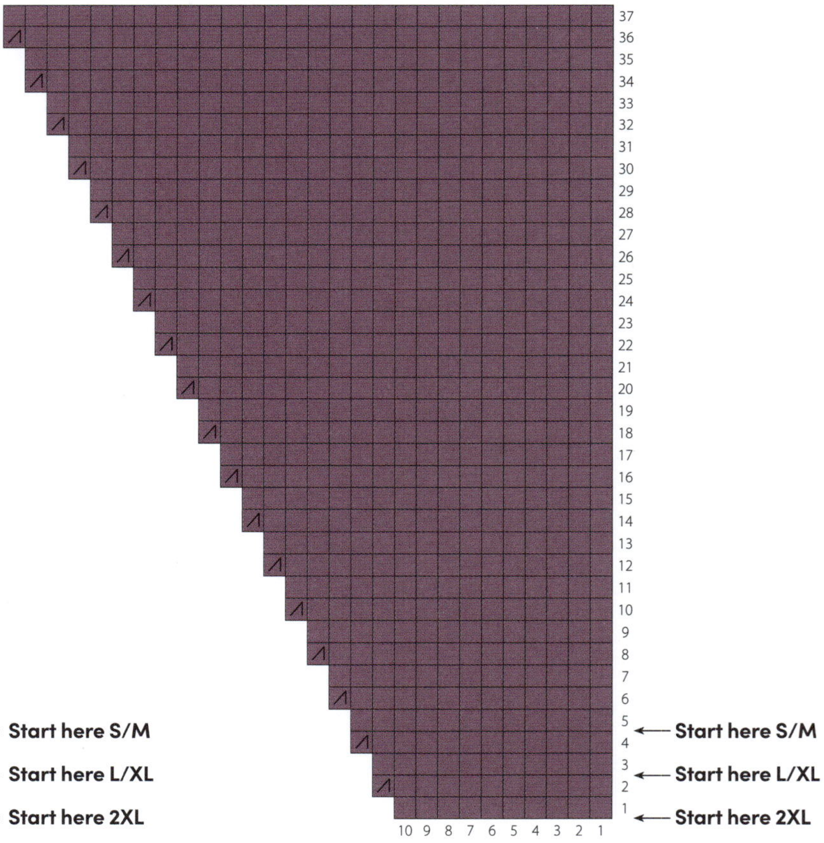

Chart D

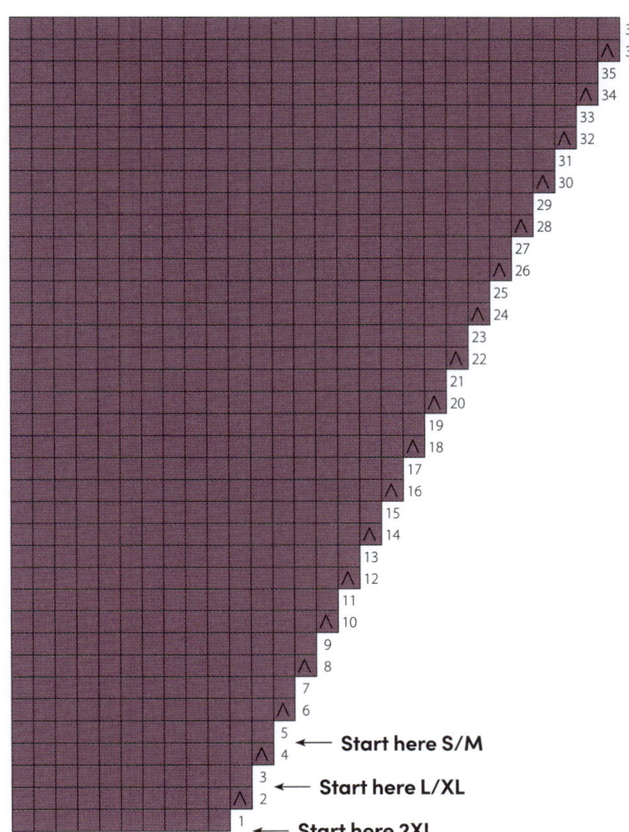

Chart E

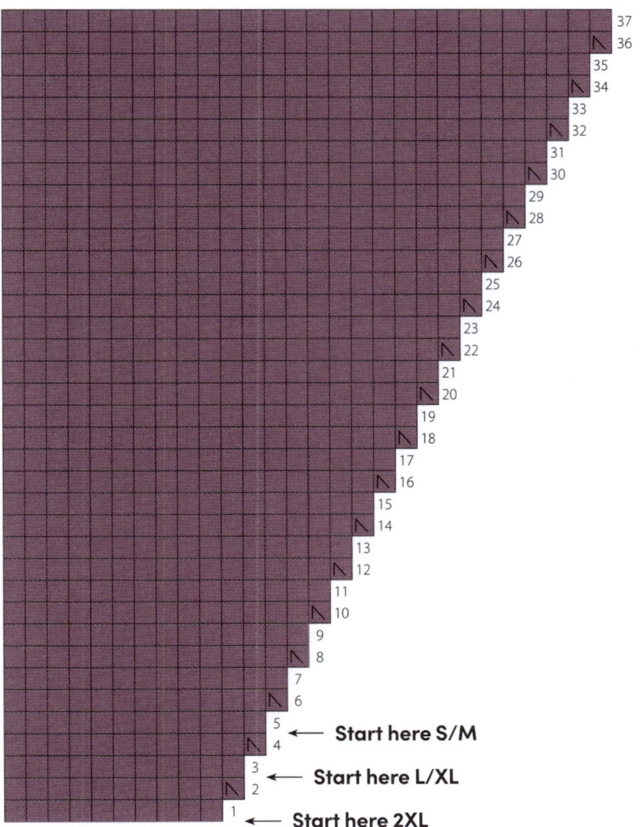

Chart F

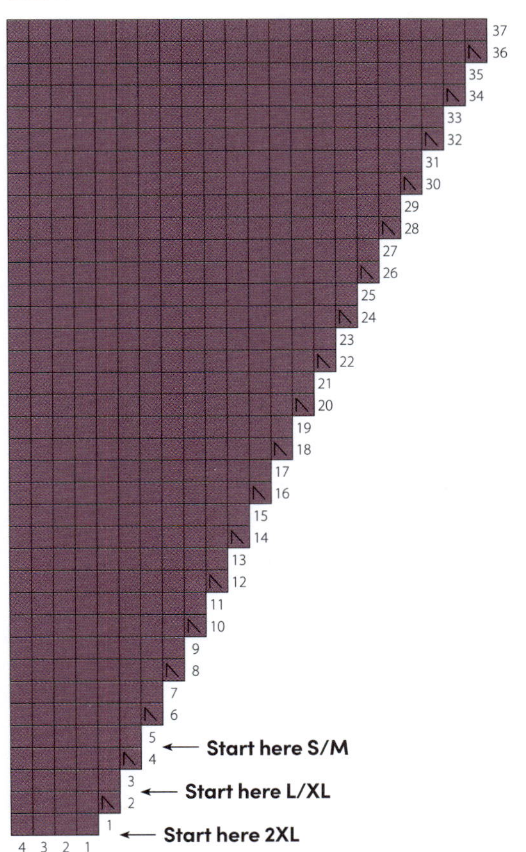

Chart G

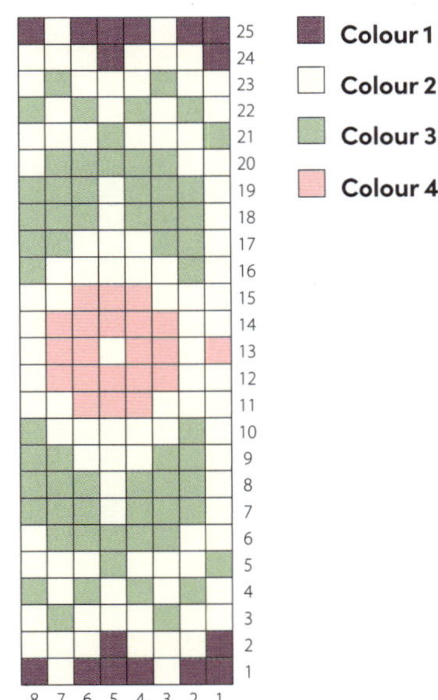

◿ = Increase slanting left (See Knitting School, page 163)

Λ = Increase in the stich below (See Knitting School, page 163)

◺ = Increase slanting right (See Knitting School, page 163)

Dahlia

SUMMER

The dahlia originated in Mexico and was brought to Europe in the 18th century. It is named after the apprentice of Carl Linnaeus, Anders Dahl. The colourful flower had its glory days in the 19th century but has, in recent years, found its way back into our hearts and our flower beds. Like here, in the dazzling Dahlia Park in Enskede, south of Stockholm.

The Dahlia cardigan is designed to be used for summer parties, weddings and family gatherings. A festive garment to wear when you want to feel extra nice and dressed up.

The Dahlia is knitted with three strands of mohair, which makes it feather light and fluffy as a cloud. You can mix the three threads in any combination you want colour wise, and that way create beautiful hues and unique blends. The cardigan's ribbed edges use an exciting technique – they are made with slipped stitches, so that you don't have to purl when knitting back and forth.

Yarn: Fin Mohair Silke from Järbo (72% mohair, 28% silk, 25g = 210 m/229 yd)
Tension: 18 sts × 24 rows in stocking stitch using 4 mm (US 6) needles = 10 × 10 cm
Sizes: XS (S) M (L) XL (2XL)
Bust: 89 (101) 110 (118) 128 (136) cm/35 (39¾) 43¼ (46½) 50½ (53½) in
Length: 54 (54) 55 (55) 56 (56) cm/21¼ (21¼) 21¾ (21¾) 22 (22) in
Sleeve length: 47 (47) 48 (48) 49 (49) cm/ 18½ (18½) 19 (19) 19¼ (19¼) in
Amounts: Colour 1 = 175 (200) 225 (250) 275 (300) g Pink Marshmallow (no. 31529)
Colour 2 = 100 (100) 125 (125) 150 (150) g Oyster Mushroom (no. 31523)
Double-pointed needles: 3.5 (US 4) and 4 mm (US 6)
Circular needles: 3.5 (US 4) and 4 mm (US 6), 80 cm
Notions: 4 stitch markers, stitch holder
Difficulty level: 2 of 3
Construction: The cardigan is knitted from the top down in one piece, with balloon sleeves. The front edges don't have any buttons or buttonholes, instead the cardigan is worn open, like a bolero.
Techniques: PM = place marker, see Knitting School, page 163.
SM = slip marker, see Knitting School, page 163.
M1R = increase 1 st slanting right, see Knitting School, page 163.
M1L = increase 1 st slanting left, see Knitting School, page 163.

RIBBED EDGE WITH SLIPPED STITCHES WHEN KNITTING BACK AND FORTH
Row 1 (RS) = knit.
Row 2 (WS) = *Slip 2 sts purlwise with the yarn in front of work, k2*. Repeat from *–* to end of row.

RIBBED EDGE WITH SLIPPED STITCHES WHEN KNITTING IN THE ROUND
Rnd 1 = knit.
Rnd 2 = *Slip 2 sts purlwise with the yarn at the back of work, p2*. Repeat from *–* to end of row.

Yoke

N.B. The whole garment is knitted with: 2 strands of colour 1 and 1 strand of colour 2 (= 3 strands in total).

With 4 mm circular needle: Cast on 48 (50) 56 (60) 64 (68) sts.

Row 1 (WS): Purl, at the same time, place stitch markers as follows: p2, PM (see Techniques), p8, PM, p28 (30) 36 (40) 44 (48), PM, p8, PM, p2.

Make raglan increases:

Row 2 (RS): k1 *Knit to last 1 st before marker, M1R (see Techniques), k1, SM (see Techniques), k1, M1L (see Techniques) *. Repeat from *–* another 3 times, k to end of row (= 8 new stitches) = 56 (58) 64 (68) 72 (76) sts.

Row 3: Purl.

Rows 4 and 5: Repeat rows 2 and 3 = 64 (66) 72 (76) 80 (84) sts. Make raglan increases, at the same time start increases for V-shaped front:

Row 6: k1, M1L, *Knit to last 1 st before marker, M1R, k1, SM, k1, M1L*. Repeat from *–* another 3 times, Knit to last 1 st, M1R, k1 (= 10 new stitches) = 74 (76) 82 (86) 90 (94) sts.

Row 7: Purl.

Repeat rows 4–7 another 9 (11) 12 (13) 14 (15) times = 236 (274) 298 (320) 342 (364) sts. Then repeat rows 4–5 another 1 (1) 1 (1) 2 (2) times = 244 (282) 306 (328) 358 (380) sts.

Divide for body and sleeves

Knit to the first stitch marker, place the following 52 (60) 64 (68) 74 (78) sts (= left sleeve) on a stitch holder/scrap yarn. Remove the first two stitch markers and cast on 6 sts for the armhole. Knit to next stitch marker, place the following 52 (60) 64 (68) 74 (78) sts (= right sleeve) on a stitch holder. Remove the last two stitch markers, cast on 6 sts for the armhole, knit to end of row = 152 (174) 190 (204) 222 (236) sts.

Body

Work in stocking stitch (= knit on right side and purl on wrong side, when knitting back and forth) until the body measures 21 (21) 22 (22) 23 (23) cm from the armhole. Finish with a wrong side row, and at the same time, decrease 2 (0) 0 (2) 0 (2) sts evenly spaced across the row = 150 (174) 190 (202) 222 (234) sts.

Change to 3.5 mm circular needle and work in rib with slipped stitches for 7 cm. (See instructions under Techniques.) N.B. On the wrong side (row 2) always k2 before you continue working in rib. Cast off knitwise.

Sleeves

Place the stitches from one of the sleeves onto 4 mm dpns.

Rnd 1: Starting at the centre of the underarm , pick up 4 new stitches (= the 3 first of the new stitches that were cast on at the underarm, and the fourth in the 'gap' in the transition between the original sleeve stitches), knit the 52 (60) 64 (68) 74 (78) sts of the sleeve, pick up 4 new stitches = 60 (68) 72 (76) 82 (86) sts.

Place stitch marker at beg of rnd.

Work in stocking stitch (= knit all rnds when knitting in the round) until the sleeve measures 38 (38) 39 (39) 40 (40) cm.

Dec rnd 1: k2 (2) 0 (2) 1 (3), *k2tog, k5* (*k2tog, k6*) *k2tog, k7* (*k2tog, k7*) *k2tog, k8* (*k2tog, k8*). Repeat from *–* to last 2 (2) 0 (2) 1 (3) sts, k2 (2) 0 (2) 1 (3) = 52 (60) 64 (68) 74 (78) sts.

Knit 1 row.

Dec rnd 2: k2 (2) 0 (2) 1 (3), *k2tog, k4* (*k2tog, k5*) *k2tog, k6*

(*k2tog, k6*) *k2tog, k7* (*k2tog, k7*). Repeat from *-* to last 2 (2) 0 (2) 1 (3) sts, k2 (2) 0 (2) 1 (3) = 44 (52) 56 (60) 66 (70) sts.

Knit 1 rnd.

Dec rnd 3: k2 (2) 0 (2) 1 (3), *k2tog, k3* (*k2tog, k4*) *k2tog, k5* (*k2tog, k5*) *k2tog, k6* (*k2tog, k6*). Repeat from *-* to last 2 (2) 0 (2) 1 (3) sts, k2 (2) 0 (2) 1 (3) = 36 (44) 48 (52) 58 (62) sts.

Knit 1 rnd, at the same time, decrease 0 (0) 4 (4) 6 (10) sts evenly spaced across the rnd = 36 (44) 44 (48) 52 (52) sts remaining on the needles.

Change to 3.5 mm dpns and work in rib with slipped stitches for 7 cm. Cast off knitwise.

Ribbed front band

With 3.5 mm circular needle and right side facing: Pick up stitches along the front edges and neck (start on the right side) and skip approximately every 4th stitch (actually corresponding to rows of front) so that you get a number of stitches that is divisible by 4 sts + 2. For example 242 (246) 250 (254) 258 (262) sts.

Work in rib with slipped stitches for 7 cm ending with WS row. (N.B. First row = Row 2/WS.)

N.B. On the wrong side the 2 first slipped stitches are replaced with k2, before you continue in in established rib pattern.

Cast off knitwise.

Finishing

Weave in loose ends. Block the cardigan carefully according to the instructions in the Knitting School, page 161.

Hortensia

SUMMER

Hortensia blue is an incredible colour. There are many stories of how the flower got its name, but for me, this is the version that has stuck: in 1766, the French botanist Philibert Commerson went for a voyage of discovery to Asia. Only men were allowed to participate, but despite this, he smuggled his dear Hortense Barré aboard. She managed this by dressing like a man and pretending to be his servant. During the journey, Hortense's true identity was exposed, but she still managed to bring back the legendary plant. The flower was named Hortensia, after Hortense.

The Hortensia vest is a useful garment with a nice finish. It's knitted with one strand of wool yarn and one strand of mohair, for extra flair.

Yarn: Svensk Ull 3-ply from Järbo (100% Swedish wool, 100 g = 180 m/196 yd) and Fin Mohair Silke from Järbo (72% mohair, 28% silk, 25 g = 210 m/ 230 yd)
Tension: 17 sts × 22 rows in stocking stitch using 4.5 mm (US 7) and both ends of yarn used together needles = 10 × 10 cm
Sizes: S (M) L (XL) 2XL (3XL)
Vest bust: 88 (96) 102 (112) 124 (136) cm/ 34¾ (37¾) 40¼ (44) 48¾ (53½) in
Vest length: 48 (49) 50 (51) 52 (53) cm/ 19 (19¼) 19¾ (20) 20½ (20¾) in
Amounts: 200 (300) 300 (300) 400 (400) g Svensk Ull 3-ply, Dala Blue (no. 59012) and 75 (75) 75 (100) 100 (100) g Fin Mohair Silke, Natural White (no. 31520)
Circular needles: 3.5 mm (US 4) and 4.5 mm (US 7), 80 cm
Double-pointed needles: 3.5 mm (US 4)
Notions: 5 buttons (approx. 25 mm), 1 wool needle for Italian cast off, 4.5 mm (US 7) dpns for 3-needle cast off, stitch holder
Difficulty level: 2 of 3
Construction: The vest is knitted back and forth in one piece from the bottom up. First the body, then the front and back. The shoulders are knitted together using the 3-needle cast off method. The ribbed edges have a nice finish with Italian cast on and cast off.
Techniques: RIBBED EDGE (RS) = the 8 first sts: slip first st knitwise, with the yarn at the back of work (p1, k1), rep twice more p1, At the end of the row, work the 8 last stitches: (p1, k1), rep 3 times more.

RIBBED EDGE (WS): the 8 first sts: slip first st purlwise, with the yarn in front of work (k1, p1) rep twice more, k1. At the end of the row work the 8 last stitches: (k1, p1), rep 3 times more.

BUTTONHOLE (RS) = slip first st knitwise, with the yarn at the back of the work, p1, k1, cast off 2 sts in knit, k1, p1.

BUTTONHOLE (WS) = work in established pattern with ribbed edge and purl to last 8 stitches, work the last 8 stitches as follows: k1, p1, k1, cast on 2 sts using the double twisted loop technique (see video links in Knitting School, page 164), p1, k1, p1.

Bottom rib

Note that the first stitch on a right-side row is always slipped knitwise with the yarn at the back of work and the first stitch on a wrong-side row is always slipped purlwise with the yarn in front of work. This way you get neat edges.

With 3.5 mm circular needle and a strand of each yarn used together: Cast on 177 (193) 205 (221) 241 (261) sts using the Italian cast on technique (see video links in Knitting School, page 164). Start and finish with k1.

Rib row 1 (WS): p1, work in rib (k1tbl, SL1pw wyif), repeat to last 2 sts, k1tbl, p1.

Rib row 2 (RS): k1, work in rib (SL1pw wyif, k1), rep to end of row.

Rib row 3: p1 (k1, SL1pw), rep to last 2 sts, k1, p1.

Rib row 4: k1 (p1, k1), rep to end of row.

Rib row 5: p1 (k1, p1), rep to end of row.

Rep rows 4 & 5 until the work measures 2.5 cm ending with a wrong-side row.

Body

Row 1 (RS): Change to 4.5 mm circular needle – work 8 sts of ribbed edge (see Techniques), knit and at the same time decrease 10 sts evenly spaced over the following 161 (177) 189 (205) 225 (245) sts. Then work ribbed edge over the final 8 sts = 167 (183) 195 (211) 231 (251) sts.

Row 2 (WS): Work 8 sts of ribbed edge, purl to last 8 sts, work ribbed edge.

Row 3: Work ribbed edge with buttonhole (see Techniques), knit to last 8 sts, work ribbed edge.

Row 4: Work 8 sts of ribbed edge, purl to last 8 sts, work ribbed edge with the second buttonhole row.

Row 5: Work 8 sts of ribbed edge, knit to last 8 sts, work ribbed edge.

Row 6: Work 8 sts of ribbed edge, purl to last 8 sts, work ribbed edge. Repeat rows 5 and 6 until the work measures 30 cm.

AT THE SAME TIME make a new buttonhole (row 3 and 4) every 20 rows – you should make 5 buttonholes in total.

Divide for armholes

Work 43 (47) 50 (53) 58 (63) sts in pattern as set with ribbed edge and stocking stitch, cast off 6 (6) 6 (8) 8 (8) m (= armhole). K69 (77) 83 (89) 99 (109) and cast off 6 (6) 6 (8) 8 (8) sts (= armhole). Work 43 (47) 50 (53) 58 (63) sts in pattern as set with stocking stitch and ribbed edge.

Now the fronts and back are knitted separately.

Left front

Continue working in pattern as set, with ribbed edge and stocking stitch. Start with a wrong-side row. Then start decreasing for the armhole:

Cast off 2 sts at the start of the right-side rows that follows 1 (1) 1 (2) 2 (2) times.

Then cast off 1 st on the right-side rows another 2 (5) 6 (7) 10 (9) times = 39 (40) 42 (42) 44 (50) sts.

AT THE SAME TIME shape a neckband when the work measures 6 cm from the armhole.

With RS of work facing:

Next row: Work 20 (20) 22 (23) 25 (25) sts then place the next 19 (20) 20 (19) 19 (25) sts on a stitch holder/scrap yarn for front neck.

Decrease for the neckband: Turn and cast off 2 sts, purl to end of row.

Continue working in stocking stitch, and cast off 1 st, 2 times at the beginning of the wrong side rows that follow = 16 (16) 18 (19) 21 (21) sts.

Knit in stocking stitch until the work measures 18 (19) 20 (21) 22 (23) cm from the armhole. Finish with a wrong-side row.

Cut the yarn and place the remaining stitches on a stitch holder.

Right front

Re-join the yarn and start decreasing for the armhole from the wrong side: Cast off 2 sts at the beginning of the wrong-side rows that follow 1 (1) 1 (2) 2 (2) times. Then cast off 1 st on the wrong-side row another 2 (5) 6 (7) 10 (9) times = 39 (40) 42 (42) 44 (50) sts.

AT THE SAME TIME, shape a neckband when the work measures 6 cm from the armhole.

With RS of work facing:

Next row: Place the next 19 (20) 20 (19) 19 (25) sts on a stitch holder. Join the yarn and then knit 20 (20) 22 (23) 25 (25) sts.

Decrease for neckband: Turn and purl one row.

Continue in stocking stitch, and cast off 2 sts, knit to end of row.

Continue in stocking stitch and cast off 1 sts, 2 times at the beginning of the following 2 knit rows = 16 (16) 18 (19) 21 (21) sts.

Work in stocking stitch until the work measures 18 (19) 20 (21) 22 (23) cm from the armhole. Finish with a wrong-side row.

Cut the yarn and place the remaining stitches on a stitch holder.

Back

With WS of work facing:

Re-join the yarn and purl 1 row. Then decrease for armholes: Cast off 2 st 1 (1) 1 (2) 2 (2) times = 65 (73) 79 (81) 91 (101) sts. Then cast off 1 st another 2 (4) 5 (5) 10 (14) times at each end = 61 (65) 69 (71) 71 (73) sts.

Continue working in stocking stitch until the work measures 16 (17) 18 (19) 20 (21) cm from the armhole. Finish with a wrong-side row.

With right side facing cast off the 27 (31) 31 (31) 27 (29) sts in the middle for the neck. Then each shoulder is finished separately.

Left shoulder

Decrease for neckline: Purl 1 row. Cast off 1 st on the next row at the neck edge = 16 (16) 18 (19) 21 (21) sts remaining for the shoulder.

Work in stocking stitch until the work measures 18 (19) 20 (21) 22 (23) cm from the armhole. Cut the yarn and place remaining stitches on a stitch holder and set aside.

Right shoulder

Decrease for neckline: Purl 1 row and cast off 1 st at neck edge = 16 (16) 18 (19) 21 (21) sts remaining for the shoulder.

Work in stocking stitch until the work measures same as left side from the armhole. Cut the yarn and place remaining stitches on a stitch holder and set aside.

Finishing

SHOULDERS

Join the shoulders by using the 3-needle cast off method (see Knitting School, page 164): Place the stitches from the right shoulder (front and back panels) onto 4.5 mm dpns.

Place the work with right sides facing, hold the needles together in the left hand and knit with a third needle in the right hand. Take 1 st from the front and 1 st from the back needle and knit the 2 sts together. Knit together the following 2 sts the same way and pass the first stitch on the right needle over the other = 1 sts remaining on the needle. Continue knitting the stitches together and cast off sts the same way. Cut the yarn and weave in loose ends. Repeat for the left shoulder.

NECKBAND

With circular needle 3.5 mm and right side facing – place the stitches put on hold for the right front onto the circular needle. Work the first 8 sts in rib (k1, p1), knit the rest of the sts. Then, pick up stitches evenly spaced across the edge (to make sure the neckband is flexible, pick up a new stitch in 3 of 4 rows), then place the stitches put on hold for the left front onto the left needle. Knit to last 8 sts, then work in rib in the pattern as set (p1, k1). N.B. The total number of stitches must be divisible by 2 + 1.

Row 2 (WS): p1, *k1, p1*, repeat from *–* to end of row.
Row 3 (RS): k1,*p1, k1*, repeat from *–* to end of row.

Work in rib (k1, p1) another 2 rows.

Then continue in rib, but for the following 2 rows, the knit stitches are knitted as usual while the purl stitches are slipped purlwise – with yarn in front of work.

From the right side: Cast off using the Italian method (see video links in Knitting School, page 164).

ARMHOLE EDGES

With 3.5 mm dpns, right side facing and starting in the middle of the underarm – pick up stitches evenly spaced across the row by picking up new stitches in 3 of 4 rows. N.B. The number of stitches must be divisible by 2. Make sure to pick up the same number of stitches around both armholes.

Work in rib in the round (k1, p1) for 5 rows. Continue in rib, but on the next row the knit stitches are knitted as usual and while the purl stitches are slipped purlwise – with yarn in front of the work.

From the right side: Cast off using the Italian method.

BUTTONS

Weave in loose ends. Block the cardigan carefully according to the instructions in the Knitting School, page 161. Sew on buttons to correspond with the buttonholes.

Fleur-de-lis

SUMMER

I have always been fascinated by symbols and their meaning. In Guldsmedshyttan's church in Bergslagen the ceiling is decorated with stars, planets and lilies – motifs that gave me the inspiration for the colourwork pattern in this cardigan.

Fleur-de-lis, the heraldic lily, is an old French symbol that, among other things, is associated with the Virgin Mary, royalty and Catholic saints.

The Fleur-de-lis cardigan is a short-sleeved summer cardigan, to wear with a skirt or dress.

Tip! If you prefer long sleeves instead you can follow the instructions in the Spring Laundry pattern (page 18).

Yarn: Svensk Ull 3-ply from Järbo (100% Swedish wool, 100 g = 180 m/196 yd)
Tension: 21 sts × 28 rows in stocking stitch in pattern using 4 mm (US 6) needles = 10 × 10 cm
Sizes: XS (S) M (L) XL (2XL) 3XL (4XL)
Bust: 80 (90) 100 (110) 120 (130) 140 (150) cm/ 31½ (35½) 39¼ (43¼) 47¼ (51¼) 55 (59) in
Length: 52 (52) 52 (53) 54 (55) 55 (56) cm/ 20½ (20½) 20½ (20¾) 21¼ (21¾) 21¾ (22) in
Sleeve length: 12 (12) 12 (13.5) 13.5 (13.5) 13.5 (13.5) cm/4¾ (4¾) 4¾ (5¼) 5¼ (5¼) 5¼ (5¼) in
Amounts: Colour 1 = 300 (300) 300 (400) 400 (400) 500 (500) g Arctic Fox (no. 59001)
Colour 2 = 25 (25) 25 (25) 25 (25) 25 (25) g Bauer Forest (no. 59019)
Double-pointed needles: 3.5 mm (US 4) and 4 mm (US 6)
Circular needles: 3.5 mm (US 4) and 4 mm (US 6), 60 cm
Notions: 10 buttons (13–15 mm), 8 stitch markers, stitch holder
Difficulty level: 2 of 3
Construction: The cardigan is knitted from the top down in once piece – with short raglan sleeves and a patterned band at the bottom.
Techniques: SM = slip marker, see Knitting School, page 163.
INCREASES, RIGHT SIDE
M1R and M1L = increases with right or left slanting: see Knitting School, page 163.
CORRESPONDING INCREASES, WRONG SIDE
M1PR = pick up the thread between 2 sts from the back with the left needle and purl through the front loop.
M1PL = pick up the thread between 2 sts from the front with the left needle and purl through the back loop.
N.B. When knitting the patterned band, don't run colour 2 along the back of the work when you get to the button bands. Instead, leave the end of the yarn hanging while knitting the ribbed edge, and then wrap it half-way around colour 1 when you continue knitting – the same technique as for intarsia knitting.

Yoke

RIBBED NECK EDGE

With circular needle 3.5 mm and colour 1: Cast on 105 (105) 105 (105) 105 (113) 113 (113) sts.

Row 1 (WS): With yarn in front of work, slip 1 st purlwise, *k1, p1*. Repeat from *–* to end of row.

Row 2: (RS): With yarn at back of work, Slip 1 st knitwise, *p1, k1*. Repeat from *–* to end of row.

Row 3: As row 1.

Row 4 (buttonhole row): As row 2 to last 4 sts, yo, k2tog, p1, k1. N.B. Make a new buttonhole the same way every 14 rows, 9 times more.

Row 5: As row 1.

Row 6: As row 2.

Row 7: As row 1. On this row you should also place 4 stitch markers (see Knitting School, page 163): between stitches 22/23 (22/23) 22/23 (22/23) 22/23 (23/24) 23/24 (23/24) = marker D. Between stitches 34/35 (34/35) 34/35 (34/35) 34/35 (37/38) 37/38 (37/38) = marker C. Between stitches 71/72 (71/72) 71/72 (71/72) 71/72 (76/77) 76/77 (76/77) = marker B. Finally, between stitches 83/84 (83/84) 83/84 (83/84) 83/84 (90/91) 90/91 (90/91) = marker A.

Now the ribbed edge is finished. Change to 4 mm circular needle and change to stocking stitch back and forth where nothing else is specified.

Row 8 (RS, Short row): Read about short rows and wrap and turn on page 162. Work the first 6 stitches in rib the same way as the ribbed edge. Knit to marker C, SM (see Techniques), k6, wrap and turn.

Row 9 (WS, Short row): Purl to marker B, SM, p6, wrap and turn.

Row 10 (RS, Short row): Knit to marker D, SM, wrap and turn. (Pick up and work wrapped stitch from previous row according to the instructions.)

Row 11 (WS, Short row): Purl to marker A, SM, wrap and turn. (Pick up and work wrapped stitch from previous row according to the instructions.)

Row 12 (RS, Short row): Knit to last 6 sts, work the last 6 sts in rib keeping pattern correct.

Row 13: Work the first 6 sts in rib as before, purl to last 6 sts, work the last 6 sts in rib as before.

Make raglan increases:

Row 14: Work 6 sts in rib, knit to last 1 st before marker A, M1R (see Techniques), k1, SM, k1, M1L (see Techniques), k10, M1R, k1, SM, k1, M1L. Knit to last 1 st before marker C, M1R, k1, SM, k1, M1L, k10, M1R, k1, SM, k1, M1L. Knit to last 6 sts, work 6 sts in rib = 8 new stitches = 113 (113) 113 (113) 113 (121) 121 (121) sts.

Row 15 (XS): Work the first 6 sts in rib as before, purl to last 6 sts, work 6 sts in rib. **(S–4XL):** Work the first 6 sts in rib, purl to last 1 st before marker D, M1PR, p1, SM, p1, MIPL. Purl to last 1 st before marker C, M1PR, p1, SM, p1, MIPL. Purl to last 1 st before marker B, M1PR, p1, SM, p1, MIPL. Purl to last 1 st before marker A, M1PR, p1, SM, p1, MIPL, purl to last 6 sts, work 6 sts in rib.

Row 16: Work 6 sts in rib, knit to last 1 st before marker A, M1R, k1, SM, k1, M1L. Knit to last 1 st before marker B, M1R, k1, SM, k1, M1L. Knit to last 1 st before marker C, M1R, k1, SM, k1, M1L. Knit to last 1 st before marker D, M1R, k1, SM, k1, M1L. Knit to last 6 sts, work 6 sts in rib = 121 (129) 129 (129) 129 (137) 137 (137) sts.

Row 17 (XS–S): Work 6 sts in rib, purl to last 6 sts, work 6 sts in rib. **(M–4XL):** Work 6 sts in rib, purl to last 1 st before marker D, M1PR, p1, SM, p1, MIPL. Purl to last 1 st before marker C, M1PR, p1, SM, p1, MIPL. Purl to last 1 st before marker B, M1PR, p1, SM, p1, MIPL. Purl to last 1 st before marker A, M1PR, p1, SM, p1, MIPL. Purl to last 6 sts, work 6 sts in rib.

Row 18 (buttonhole row): Work 6 sts in rib, knit to last 1 st before marker A, M1R, k1, SM, k1, M1L. Knit to last 1 st before marker B, M1R, k1, SM, k1, M1L. Knit to last 1 st before marker C, M1R, k1, SM, k1, M1L. Knit to last 1 st before marker D, M1R, k1, SM, k1, M1L. Knit to last 6 sts, work 6 sts in rib, making buttonhole as before.

Row 19 (XS–S): Work 6 sts in rib, purl to last 6 sts, work 6 sts in rib. **(M–4XL):** Work the first 6 sts in rib, purl to last 1 st before marker D, M1PR, p1, SM, p1, MIPL. Purl to last 1 st before marker C, M1PR, p1, SM, p1, MIPL. Purl to last 1 st before marker B, M1PR, p1, SM, p1, MIPL. Purl to last 1 st before marker A, M1PR, p1, SM, p1, MIPL. Purl to last 6 sts, work 6 sts in rib.

Row 20: As row 18.

Row 21 (XS–M): Work the first 6 sts in rib, purl to last 6 sts, work the last 6 sts in rib. **(L–4XL):** Work 6 sts in rib, purl to last 1 st before marker D, M1PR, p1, SM, p1, MIPL. Purl to last 1 st before marker C, M1PR, p1, SM, p1, MIPL. Purl to last 1 st before marker B, M1PR, p1, SM, p1, MIPL. Purl to last 1 st before marker A, M1PR, p1, SM, p1, MIPL. Purl to last 6 sts, work 6 sts in rib.

Row 22: As row 18.

Row 23: As row 21.

Row 24: As row 18.

Row 25 (XS–M): Work 6 sts in rib, purl to last 6 sts, work 6 sts in rib. **(L–4XL):** Work 6 sts in rib, purl to last 1 st before marker D, M1PR, p1, SM, p1, MIPL. Purl to last 1 st before marker C, M1PR, p1, SM, p1, MIPL. Purl to last 1 st before marker B, M1PR, p1, SM, p1, MIPL. Purl to last 1 st before marker A, M1PR, p1, SM, p1, MIPL. Purl to last 6 sts, work 6 sts in rib.

Row 26: As row 18.

Row 27 (XS–L): Work 6 sts in rib, purl to last 6 sts, work 6 sts in rib. **(XL–4XL):** Work 6 sts in rib, purl to last 1 st before marker D, M1PR, p1, SM, p1, MIPL. Purl to last 1 st before marker C, M1PR, p1, SM, p1, MIPL. Purl to last 1 st before marker B, M1PR, p1, SM, p1, MIPL. Purl to last 1 st before marker A, M1PR, p1, SM, p1, MIPL. Purl to last 6 sts, work 6 sts in rib.

Row 28: As row 18.

Row 29: As row 27.

Row 30: As row 18.

Row 31 (XS–XL): Work 6 sts in rib, purl to last 6 sts, work 6 sts in rib. **(2XL–4XL):** Work the first 6 sts in rib, purl to last 1 st before marker D, M1PR, p1, SM, p1, MIPL. Purl to last 1 st before marker C, M1PR, p1, SM, p1, MIPL. Purl to last 1 st before marker B, M1PR, p1, SM, p1, MIPL. Purl to last 1 st before marker A, M1PR, p1, SM, p1, MIPL. Purl to last 6 sts, work 6 sts in rib.

Row 32 (buttonhole row): As row 18.

Row 33 (XS–2XL): Work 6 sts in rib, purl to last 6 sts, work 6 sts in rib. **(3XL–4XL):** Work 6 sts in rib, purl to last 1 st before marker D, M1PR, p1, SM, p1, MIPL. Purl to last 1 st before marker C, M1PR, p1, SM, p1, MIPL. Purl to last 1 st before marker B, M1PR, p1, SM, p1, MIPL. Purl to last 1 st before marker A, M1PR, p1, SM, p1, MIPL. Purl to last 6 sts, work 6 sts in rib.

Row 34: As row 18.

Row 35 (XS–2XL): Work 6 sts in rib, purl to last 6 sts, work 6 sts in rib. **(3XL–4XL):** Work 6 sts in rib, purl to last 1 st before marker D, M1PR, p1, SM, p1, MIPL. Purl to last 1 st before marker C,

M1PR, p1, SM, p1, MIPL. Purl to last 1 st before marker B, M1PR, p1, SM, p1, MIPL. Purl to last 1 st before marker A, M1PR, p1, SM, p1, MIPL. Purl to last 6 sts, work 6 sts in rib.
Row 36: As row 18.
Row 37 (XS–3XL): Work 6 sts in rib, purl to last 6 sts, work 6 sts in rib. **(4XL):** Work 6 sts in rib, purl to last 1 st before marker D, M1PR, p1, SM, p1, MIPL. Purl to last 1 st before marker C, M1PR, p1, SM, p1, MIPL. Purl to last 1 st before marker B, M1PR, p1, SM, p1, MIPL. Purl to last 1 st before marker A, M1PR, p1, SM, p1, MIPL. Purl to last 6 sts, work 6 sts in rib.
Row 38: As row 18.
Row 39: As row 37.
Row 40: As row 18.
Row 41: Work 6 sts in rib, purl to last 6 sts, work 6 sts in rib.
Row 42: As row 18.
Row 43: As row 41.
Row 44: As row 18.
Row 45: As row 41.
Row 46 (buttonhole row): As row 18.
Row 47: As row 41.
Row 48: As row 18.
Row 49: As row 41.
Row 50: As row 18.
Row 51: As row 41.
Row 52: As row 18.
Row 53: As row 41.

Now the raglan increases for **XL–4XL** are complete. Total number of increases 28 **(XL)**, 29 **(2XL)** 31 **(3XL)** 33 **(4XL)** = 329 sts **(XL)**, 345 sts **(2XL)**, 361 sts **(3XL)**, 377 sts **(4XL)**.

Sizes **XS** to **L** only:
Row 54 (XS–L): As row 18.
Row 55: Work 6 sts in rib, purl to last 6 sts, work 6 sts in rib. Now the raglan increases for size **L** are complete. 27 increases in total = 321 sts.
Row 56 (XS–M): As row 18.
Row 57: Work 6 sts in rib, purl to last 6 sts, work 6 sts in rib.
Row 58 (XS–M): As row 18.
Row 59: Work 6 sts in rib, purl to last 6 sts, work 6 sts in rib.

Now the raglan increases for size **M** are complete. 26 increases in total = 313 sts.
Row 60 (buttonhole row): As row 18.
Row 61: Work 6 sts in rib, purl to last 6 sts, work 6 sts in rib.

Now the raglan increases for **XS–S** are complete. 24 **(XS)** and 25 **(S)** increases in total = 297 sts **(XS)**, 305 sts **(S)**.

All sizes:

Continue increasing for the body by repeating rows 1–2 below, a total of 1 (4) 7 (10) 13 (14) 15 (16) times remembering to work buttonholes every 14 rows.
Row 1: Work 6 sts in rib, knit to last 1 st before marker A, M1R, k1, SM. Knit to marker B, SM, k1, M1L. Knit to last 1 st before marker C, M1R, k1, SM. Knit to marker D, SM, k1, M1L. Knit to last 6 sts, work 6 sts in rib.
Row 2: Work 6 sts in rib, purl to last 6 sts, 6 sts in rib. When all increases are done you should have 301 (321) 341 (361) 381 (401) 421 (441) sts on the needle.

Divide for body and sleeves

Row 1 RS: Work 46 (50) 54 (58) 62 (66) 69 (72) sts keeping ribbed edge sts correct (right front), SM, place next 62 (64) 66 (68) 70 (72) 76 (80) sts on a stitch holder/scrap yarn (= right sleeve), remove marker. Knit next 85 (93) 101 (109) 117 (125) 131 (137) sts (= back), SM, place next 62 (64) 66 (68) 70 (72) 76 (80) sts on a stitch holder (left sleeve), remove marker. Work last 46 (50) 54 (58) 62 (66) 69 (72) sts keeping ribbed edge sts correct (= left front).

Now 177 (193) 209 (225) 241 (257) 269 (281) sts remain on the needle.
Row 2: Work 6 sts in rib, purl to last 6 sts, work 6 sts in rib.

Body

Row 1: Work 6 sts in rib, knit to last 6 sts, work 6 sts in rib.
Row 2: Work 6 sts in rib, purl to last 6 sts, work 6 sts in rib.
Repeat rows 1 and 2 until the work measures 15 cm from the division. Finish with a wrong-side row.

Work the colour pattern according to the chart, rows 1–22. (Continue working in rib stitch, as before, on the first and last 6 sts of the row.)

Place the pattern accordingly:

XS – Work stitches 3–28, then repeat stitches (1–28) 4 times, finish with stitches 1–27.

S – Work stitches 2–8, then repeat stitches (1–28) 5 times, finish with stitches 1–14.

M – Work stitches (1–28) 7 times, finish with stitch 1.

L – Work stitches 28, then repeat stitches (1–28) 7 times, finish with stitches 1–16.

XL – Work stitches 27–28, then repeat stitches (1–28) 8 times, finish with stitches 1–3.

2XL – Work stitches 26–28, then repeat stitches (1–28) 8 times, finish with stitches 1–18.

3XL – Work stitches 27–28, then repeat stitches (1–28) 9 times, finish with stitches 1–3.

4XL – Work stitches 28, then repeat stitches (1–28) 9 times, finish with stitches 1–16.

Follow the chart from right to left on a right-side row and in the opposite direction on a wrong side row.

With colour 1: Finish with two rows in stocking stitch with established rib.

Change to 3.5 mm circular needle and work in rib (k1, p1 – with slipped stitch at the beginning of the row as before) for 5 cm. Finish with a wrong-side row. Cast off loosely in rib.

Sleeves

Divide the 62 (64) 66 (68) 70 (72) 76 (80) sts from one sleeve over 4 mm dpns, as evenly as possible. Join the yarn by picking up 1 st under the sleeve, k62 (64) 66 (68) 70 (72) 76 (80), pick up another 1 st under the sleeve, place a stitch marker to mark the starting point of the rnd = 64 (66) 68 (70) 72 (74) 78 (82) sts.

Sizes **XS–M:** Knit 15 rnds in stocking stitch. Then decrease 10 sts evenly spaced across the rnd. Then work in rib (k1, p1) for 6 cm. Cast off loosely in rib.

Sizes **L–4XL:** Knit 19 rnds in stocking stitch. Then decrease 8 sts evenly spaced across the rnd. Then work in rib (k1, p1) in 6 cm. Cast off loosely in rib.

Finishing

Weave in loose ends. Block the cardigan according to page 161. Sew on buttons to correspond with buttonholes.

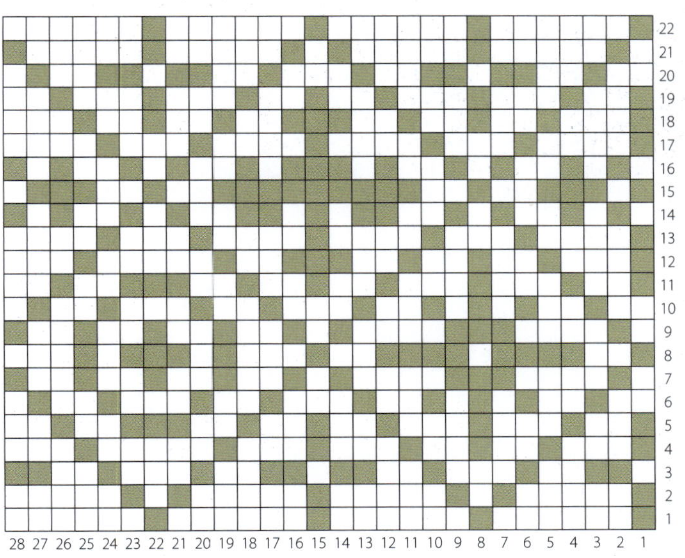

Colour 1

Colour 2

When **autumn** approaches I start to get excited – the knitter's peak season has arrived!

I indulge in rustic wool yarns and curl up in the armchair while the wind is whistling outside. This is when my projects for autumn and winter are planned and cast on – colours need to be picked and matched together for cardigans, gloves and socks. In other words, this time of year is full of busy days in the knitting workshop. It's probably always been like this and I can sense a deep nostalgia in the air. It's as if the connection between myself and earlier generations becomes stronger in the autumn darkness.

Sometimes I go out for autumnal walks and enjoy the magnificent colours that shift from day to day. The autumn leaves are whirling and the air is fresh. In the forest we pick chanterelles in the damp moss. The dahlias are flowering in the garden late into the autumn and apple sauce is bubbling away in a pan.

Autumn without cardigans would be lacking. Both wearing them and knitting them bring even deeper enjoyment to this season.

Martall

AUTUMN

A *martall* is a pine tree that grows in inaccessible and exposed places, such as windswept beaches and rocks with poor soil. Because of their conditions they end up gnarled, twisted and small in size, but they do develop unusually dense wood. In the past, it was believed that these dwarf trees had fallen victim to the *mare* – a creature in Nordic folklore who came out during the night taking the form of a woman.

A *martall* was regarded as possessing magical powers, and having the ability to cure illness, but those who felled such a tree could risk taking on all the evil that had been stored inside.

The *martall* cardigan will protect you from the cold and will carry you through testing times. In the pockets you can gather pine cones, beautiful stones and other treasures.

Yarn: Léttlopi from Ístex (100% Icelandic wool, 50 g = 100 m/109 yd)
Tension: 18 sts × 24 rows in stocking stitch in pattern using 5 mm (US 8) needles = 10 × 10 cm
Sizes: XS (S) M (L) XL (2XL) 3XL (4XL)
Bust: 85 (94) 98 (107) 120 (134) 143 (156) cm/ 33½ (37) 38½ (42¼) 47¼ (52¾) 56¼ (61½) in
Length: 55 (55.5) 59 (60) 63 (64.5) 66.5 (68) cm/21¾ (21¾) 23¼ (23½) 24¾ (25½) 26¼ (26¾) in
Sleeve length: 44 (45) 47 (49) 51 (52) 52 (52) cm/17¼ (17¾) 18½ (19¼) 20 (20½) 20½ (20½) in
Amounts: Colour 1 = 400 (450) 500 (550) (550) 600 (650) (650) g Light Beige Heather (no. 10086)
Colour 2 = 50 (50) 50 (100) 100 (100) 150 (150) g Chocolate Heather (no. 10867)
Double-pointed needles: 4.5 mm (US 7) and 5 mm (US 8)
Circular needles: 4.5 mm (US 7) and 5 mm (US 8), 80 cm
Notions: 11 buttons (15 mm in diameter), stitch holder, decorative band (optional)
Difficulty level: 3 of 3
Construction: Body and sleeves are knitted in the round separately from the bottom and up and are then joined together on one circular needle. Then the yoke is knitted with decreases, back short rows as well as a neckband. To finish, the cardigan is cut open (see Knitting School, page 160) after button bands, pocket edges and pocket bags are knitted on. N.B. The rib at the bottom and top are knitted back and forth.
Techniques: M1L = increase 1 st slanting left, see Knitting School, page 163.
M1R = increase 1 st slanting right, see Knitting School, page 163.

Body

With 4.5 mm circular needle and colour 1: Cast on 146 (162) 174 (190) 214 (234) 250 (274) sts.

Work in rib back and forth:

Row 1 (WS): *p2, k2*, repeat from *-* to last 2 sts, p2.
Row 2 (RS): *k2, p2*, repeat from *-* to last 2 sts, k2.
Row 3 (WS): *p2, k2*, repeat from *-* to last 2 sts, p2.

Repeat rows 2 and 3 until the rib measures 5 cm. N.B. Finish the rib with a wrong side.

From now on the body is knitted in the round in stocking stitch (= knit all rows when knitting in the round).

First row, with 5 mm needle: Knit and at the same time increase 7 (7) 3 (3) 3 (7) 7 (7) sts evenly spaced across the row = 153 (169) 177 (193) 217 (241) 257 (281) sts.

Then, cast on 5 steek stitches using the double twisted loop technique (see video links in the Knitting School, page 164). The steek stitches also work as a 'marker' for the beginning and end of a rnd. (N.B. The steek stitches don't count towards the cardigan's total stitch count, and any increases or decreases should not be made within these stitches.)

Join into rnd, taking care not to twist sts.

Knit 1 rnd.

Work the colour pattern according to the chart, following chart from right to left every row rnds 1–13 with following placement for each size: **XS:** knit stitches 21–24, stitches 1–24 six times in total, then stitches 1–5. (**S:** knit stitches 1–24 seven times in total, then stitch 1.) **M:** knit stitches 21–24, stitches 1–24 seven times in total, then stitches 1–5. (**L:** knit stitches 1–24 eight times in total, then stitch 1.) **XL:** knit stitches 1–24 nine times in total, then stitch 1. (**2XL:** knit stitches 1–24 ten times in total, then stitch 1.) **3XL:** knit stitches 17–24, stitches 1–24 ten times in total, then stitches 1–9. (**4XL:** knit stitches 17–24, stitches 1–24 eleven times in total, then stitches 1–9.)

With colour 1: Knit 3 rnds.

Prepare for pockets

K8 (8) 8 (12) 12 (16) 16 (20), *take a length of scrap yarn and knit the following 18 stitches with it (here the pocket will be placed later). Then go back and knit the 18 stitches once more, but now using the original yarn*. Knit to last 26 (26) 26 (30) 30 (34) 34 (38) sts on the rnd. Repeat from *-*. Knit to end of rnd.

Knit until the body measures 33 (34) 35 (36) 37 (38) 39 (40) cm or length of your choice. Set the work aside.

Sleeves

With dpns 4.5 mm and colour 1: Cast on 40 (40) 40 (40) 40 (44) 44 (44) sts.

Work in the round in rib stitch (k2, p2) for 5 cm.

From now on, knit in the round in stocking stitch (= knit all rows when knitting in the round). Change to 5 mm dpns, knit and increase 8 (8) 8 (8) 8 (4) 4 (4) sts evenly spaced across the rnd = 48 (48) 48 (48) 48 (48) 48 (48) sts.

Knit 1 rnd, placing marker at beg of rnd.

Knit the pattern according to the chart (stitches 1–24 are repeated 2 times) for 13 rows.

With colour 1: Knit 2 rnds.

Increase rnd: * k1, M1L (see Techniques), knit to last 1 stitch on the rnd, M1R (see Techniques), k1.

Knit 19 (13) 9 (7) 5 (3) 3 (3) rnds.*

Repeat from *-* 2 (4) 6 (10) 14 (18) 21 (23) times in total = 52 (56) 60 (68) 76 (84) 90 (94) sts.

Knit until the sleeve measures 44 (45) 47 (49) 51 (52) 52 (52) cm or length of your choice.

Next rnd: Knit to last 4 (5) 5 (6) 7 (7) 8 (8) sts on the rnd, place the following 8 (10) 10 (12) 14 (14) 16 (16) sts on a stitch holder/scrap yarn (= armhole stitches).

Cut the yarn and place the sleeve's remaining 44 (46) 50 (56) 62 (70) 74 (78) sts on a stitch holder. Set the work aside and make a second sleeve the same way.

Join body and sleeves

Continue knitting in the round in stocking stitch (= knit all rows when knitting in the round).

With circular needle 5 mm and colour 1: Knit the right front 34 (37) 39 (42) 47 (53) 56 (62) sts. Place the following 8 (10) 10 (12) 14 (14) 16 (16) sts on a stitch holder. Knit the right sleeve 44 (46) 50 (56) 62 (70) 74 (78) sts. Knit the back 69 (75) 79 (85) 95 (107) 113 (125) sts. Place the following 8 (10) 10 (12) 14 (14) 16 (16) sts on a stitch holder. Knit the left sleeve 44 (46) 50 (56) 62 (70) 74 (78) sts. Knit the left front 34 (37) 39 (42) 47 (53) 56 (62) sts = 225 (241) 257 (281) 313 (353) 373 (405) sts on the needle.

Knit 1 rnd.

Next rnd, sizes **XS, S, M, 2XL:** knit. Sizes **L, XL, 3XL, 4XL:** decrease 8 (8) 4 (4) sts evenly spaced = 225 (241) 257 (273) 305 (353) 369 (401) sts on the needle.

Yoke

Knit 11 (12) 13 (14) 16 (17) 18 (19) rnds.

Dec rnd 1: k1, *k6, k2tog*. Repeat from *-* To end of row.

Knit 8 rnds.

Dec rnd 2: k7, *k2tog, k12*. Repeat from *-* to last 8 sts on the rnd, k2tog, k6.

Knit 11 rnds.

Dec rnd 3: k2, *k2tog, k11*. Repeat from *-* to last 12 sts on the rnd, k2tog, k10.

Knit 2 rnds.

Dec rnd 4: k3, *k2tog, k4*. Repeat from *-* to last 4 sts on the rnd, k2tog, k2.

Knit 5 rnds.

Dec rnd 5: k3, *k2tog, k3*. Repeat from *-* to last 3 sts on the rnd, k2tog, k1.

Knit 2 rnds.

Dec rnd 6: k2, *k2tog, k2*. Repeat from *-* to last 3 sts on the rnd, k2tog, k1 = 85 (91) 97 (103) 115 (133) 139 (151) sts on the needle.

Back short rows

Read about short rows and wrap and turn on page 162. Now you will knit stocking stitch back and forth with knit and purl short rows: K56 (60) 64 (68) 76 (88) 92 (100), wrap and turn. P28 (30) 32 (34) 38 (44) 46 (50), wrap and turn. *Knit to last 4 sts before the turning, wrap and turn. Purl to last 4 sts before the turning, wrap and turn*.

Repeat from *-* 2 (2) 3 (3) 4 (4) 5 (5) times in total, then, work to end of row at the same time as you pick up the wrapped stitches according to the description in the Knitting School. Knit 1 row where the remainder of the wrapped stitches are picked up and knitted.

Neckband

Decrease 3 (1) 3 (1) 1 (11) 13 (21) sts evenly spaced across the next rnd = 82 (90) 94 (102) 114 (122) 126 (130) sts.

Change to 4.5 mm circular needle and cast off the 5 steek stitches at the middle of the front.

Work in rib back and forth:

Row 1 (RS): *k2, p2*, repeat from *–* to last 2 sts, k2.
Row 2 (WS): *p2, k2*, repeat from *–* to last 2 sts, p2.

Repeat rows 1 and 2 until the rib measures 4 cm. Finish with a wrong-side row.

Dec row: *k2, p2tog*. Repeat from *–* to last 2 sts, k2 = 62 (68) 71 (77) 86 (92) 95 (98) sts. Cast off loosely in rib.

Join sleeve and body underarm

With 3.5 mm dpns: Join the stitches underneath the armholes together using the 3-needle cast off method (see Knitting School, page 164). Weave in loose ends.

Button bands

LEFT BUTTON BAND

With 4.5 mm circular needle and colour 1 (RS): Pick up stitches along the left front edge starting from the top. To make the edge flexible, pick up from 2 out of 3 rows from the front edge (= *knit 2 sts, skip the 3rd st*, repeat from *–*). Make sure the number of stitches is divisible by 4+2 sts.

Now work in rib stitch:

Row 1 (WS): *p2, k2*, repeat from *–* to last 2 sts, p2.
Row 2 (RS): *k2, p2*, repeat from *–* to last 2 sts, k2.
Row 3 (WS): *p2, k2*, repeat from *–* to last 2 sts, p2.

Repeat rows 2 and 3 four times in total (= 9 rows in total).

Cast off in rib.

RIGHT BUTTON BAND

With circular needle 4.5 mm and colour 1 (RS): Pick up stitches along the right front edge starting from the bottom. Make sure to pick up the same number of stitches as on the left side. Distribute 11 buttonholes evenly across the edge placing markers on the needle. (Each buttonhole goes over 2 sts.)

Work in rib according to the description for the left button band to row 3.

Row 4 (buttonhole row 1, RS): Work in rib to the first buttonhole. Then work as follows: *Cast off 2 sts, continue in rib as set to the next buttonhole*. Repeat from *–* until you have completed all buttonholes, then work in rib to end of row.

Row 5 (buttonhole row 2, WS): Work in rib to the first buttonhole and finish as follows: *Cast on 2 sts using the double twisted loop technique, continue in rib to the next buttonhole*. Repeat from *–* until all buttonholes have been finished then work in rib to end of row.

Work another 4 rows in rib and then cast off in rib.

Pockets (work 2 the same)

Pick up the top and bottom stitches on two 4.5 mm dpns. Carefully remove the guide thread.

With colour 1: Work in rib back and forth over the bottom 18 sts:

Row 1 (RS): Knit.
Row 2 (WS): p2, *k2, p2*, repeat from *–* to end of row.

Row 3: k2, *p2, k2*, repeat from *–* to end of row.
Row 4: p2, *k2, p2*, repeat from *–* to end of row. Repeat rows 3 and 4 until the ribbed edge measures 3 cm.

Finish with a wrong-side row. Cast off in rib from the right side. Then knit the pocket bag over the top 18 sts with 5 mm needles and colour 1: Back and forth in stocking stitch (*knit 1 row, purl 1 row*), repeat from *–* until the pocket bag measures 7 cm. Finish with a wrong side row and then cast off.

Sew the pocket bag in place carefully, along the sides and the bottom. N.B. Use colour 1 to prevent the stitches becoming visible on the right side. Then sew the sides of the ribbed edges to the right side with colour 1. Kitchener stitch is recommended. Repeat the procedure for the second pocket.

Cutting the steek

See Knitting School, page 160. Sew a reinforcing seam with sewing thread (by hand using backstitch) on each side of the middle steek stitch. Carefully cut the cardigan open in the middle of the middle steek stitch. (The cut edges will roll in towards the wrong side.)

Finishing

Weave in loose ends. Block the cardigan carefully according to the instructions in the Knitting School. Either cover the cut edges on the inside with a decorative band, or fold them in and sew with discreet stitches to the wrong side (see Knitting School, pages 160–161).

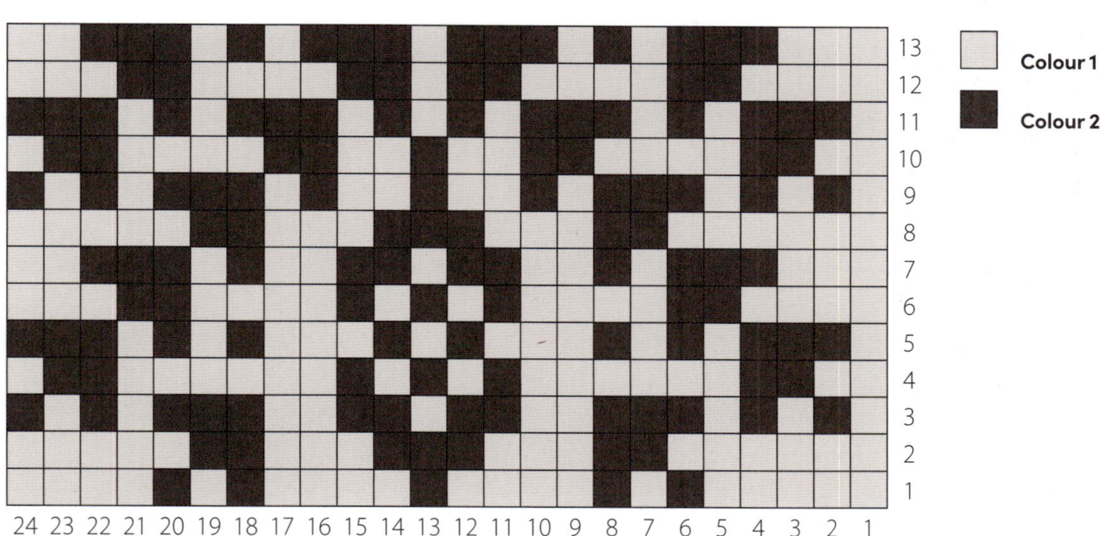
Colour 1
Colour 2

Sundborn

AUTUMN

In Sundborn you'll find Lilla Hyttnäs – Karin and Carl Larsson's extraordinary artists' home. Spending time in the rooms and studying the colours and patterns is one of the most inspiring things I have experienced. Karin Larsson's textile artworks constantly bring new perspectives to what is possible to express using needle, thread and yarn.

For the Sundborn cardigan I have let unexpected hues marry together, inspired by Karin Larsson's inimitable colour combinations. You can challenge yourself by trying out new exciting colour combinations for the yoke pattern.

Yarn: Léttlopi from Ístex (100% Icelandic wool, 50 g = 100 m/109 yd) and Vandre from Rauma Ullvarefabrikk (100% Norwegian wool, 50 g = 120 m)
Tension: 18 sts × 24 rows in stocking stitch in pattern using 5 mm (US 8) needles = 10 × 10 cm
Sizes: XS (S) M (L) XL (2XL) 3XL (4XL)
Bust: 85 (94) 98 (107) 120 (134) 143 (156) cm/ 33½ (37) 38½ (42¼) 47¼ (52¾) 56¼ (61½) in
Length: 55 (55.5) 59 (60) 63 (64.5) 66.5 (68) cm/21¾ (21¾) 23¼ (23½) 24¾ (25½) 26¼ (26¾) in
Sleeve length: 44 (45) 47 (49) 51 (52) 52 (52) cm/17¼ (17¾) 18½ (19¼) 20 (20½) 20½ (20½) in
Amounts: Colour 1 = 350 (400) 450 (500) (500) 550 (600) (600) g Léttlopi (Ístex), Black Heather (no. 10005)
Colour 2 = 100 (100) 100 (100) 100 (100) 100 (100) g Léttlopi, Golden Heather (no. 19426)
colour 3 = 50 (50) 50 (50) 50 (50) 50 (50) Vandre (Rauma), Skogsbær (no. 14123)
Double-pointed needles: 4.5 mm (US 7) and 5 mm (US 8)
Circular needles: 4.5 mm (US 7) and 5 mm (US 8), 80 cm
Notions: 5 or 9 buttons (18 mm in diameter) depending on how dense buttoning you want, stitch holder, decorative band (optional)
Difficulty level: 3 of 3
Construction: Body and sleeves are knitted in the round separately from the bottom up and are then joined together on one circular needle. Then the yoke is knitted with a colourwork pattern, decreases, back short rows and a neckband. To finish, the cardigan is cut open (see Knitting School, page 160) after button bands are knitted in. Note that the rib at the bottom and top are knitted back and forth.
Techniques: M1L = increase 1 st slanting left, see Knitting School, page 163.
M1R = increase 1 st slanting right, see Knitting School, page 163.

Body

With 4.5 mm circular needle and colour 1: Cast on 146 (162) 174 (190) 214 (234) 250 (274) sts.

Work in rib back and forth:

Row 1 (WS): *p2, k2*, repeat from *-* to last 2 sts, p2.
Row 2 (RS): *k2, p2*, repeat from *-* to last 2 sts, k2.
Row 3 (WS): *p2, k2*, repeat from *-* to last 2 sts, p2.

Repeat rows 2 and 3 until the rib measures 5 cm. N.B. Finish the rib on a wrong side row.

From now the body is knitted in the round in stocking stitch (= knit all rows when knitting in the round).

Using 5 mm needle: Knit and at the same time increase 7 (7) 3 (3) 3 (7) 7 (7) sts evenly spaced across the row = 153 (169) 177 (193) 217 (241) 257 (281) sts.

Then cast on 5 steek stitches using the double twisted loop technique (see video links in the Knitting School, page 164). The steek stitches also work as a 'marker' for the beginning and end of a row. (N.B. The steek stitches don't count towards the cardigan's total stitch count, and any increases or decreases should not be made within these stitches.)

Join into round taking care not to twist sts.

Continue in stocking stitch (= knit all rows when knitting in the round) until the body measures 25 (26) 27 (28) 29 (30) 31 (32) cm or length of your choice. Set the work aside.

Sleeves

With 4.5 mm dpns and colour 2: Cast on 40 (40) 40 (40) 40 (44) 44 (44) sts.

Work rib stitch in the round (k2, p2) for 5 cm.

Change to 5 mm dpns: Continue in stocking stitch (knit every rnd), at the same time increase 8 (8) 8 (8) 8 (4) 4 (4) sts evenly spaced across the row = 48 (48) 48 (48) 48 (48) 48 (48) sts.

Knit another 1 rnd. Place marker for beg of rnd.

Work the pattern according to the chart A (stitches 1–6 are repeated 8 times in total) for 14 rnds.

With colour 1: Knit 2 rnds.

Increase rnd: *k1, M1L (see Techniques), knit to last 1 stitch in the rnd, M1R (see Techniques), k1.

Knit 19 (13) 9 (7) 5 (3) 3 (2) rnds without increases.*

Repeat from *-* 2 (4) 6 (10) 14 (18) 21 (23) times in total = 52 (56) 60 (68) 76 (84) 90 (94) sts.

Knit until the sleeve measures 44 (45) 47 (49) 51 (52) 52 (52) cm or length of your choice.

Next rnd: Knit to last 4 (5) 5 (6) 7 (7) 8 (8) sts on the rnd. Place the following 8 (10) 10 (12) 14 (14) 16 (16) sts on a stitch holder/scrap yarn (= armhole stitches).

Cut the yarn and place the sleeve's remaining 44 (46) 50 (56) 62 (70) 74 (78) sts on a stitch holder. Set the work aside and make a second sleeve the same way.

Join body and sleeves

Continue knitting in the round in stocking stitch (= knit all rows when knitting in the round).

With circular needle 5 mm and colour 1: Knit the right front 34 (37) 39 (42) 47 (53) 56 (62) sts. Place the following 8 (10) 10 (12) 14 (14) 16 (16) sts on a stitch holder. Knit the right sleeve 44 (46) 50 (56) 62 (70) 74 (78) sts. Knit the back 69 (75) 79 (85) 95 (107) 113 (125) sts. Place the following 8 (10) 10 (12) 14 (14) 16 (16) sts on a stitch holder. Knit the left sleeve 44 (46) 50 (56) 62 (70) 74 (78) sts. Knit the left front 34 (37) 39 (42) 47 (53) 56 (62) sts = 225 (241) 257 (281) 313 (353) 373 (405) sts.

Knit 1 rnd.

Next rnd, sizes **XS**, **S**, **M**, **2XL:** K. Sizes **L**, **XL**, **3XL**, **4XL:** Decrease 8 (8) 4 (4) sts evenly spaced = 225 (241) 257 (273) 305 (353) 369 (401) sts on the needle.

Yoke

Knit 5 rnds.

Work the pattern with decreases indicated in chart B1, rnds 1–46, according to size placement below. (Depending on the size each rnd ends with either chart B2 or B3.)

Sizes **XS**, **M**, **2XL:** Repeat stitches (1–32) 6 (7) 10 times, then knit stitches 1–30 then end with stitches 1–3 in chart B2.

Sizes **S**, **L**, **XL**, **3XL**, **4XL:** Knit stitches 25–32, then repeat stitches (1–32) (7) (8) 9 11 (12) times, then knit stitches 1–6 then end with stitches 1–3 in chart B3 = 85 (91) 97 (103) 115 (133) 139 (151) stitches.

Back short rows

Read about short rows and wrap and turn on page 162. Now you will knit stocking stitch back and forth with knit and purl short rows: Knit 56 (60) 64 (68) 76 (88) 92 (100), wrap and turn. Purl 28 (30) 32 (34) 38 (44) 46 (50), wrap and turn. *Knit to last 4 sts before the turning, wrap and turn. Purl to last 4 sts before the turning, wrap and turn*.

Repeat *-* 2 (2) 3 (3) 4 (4) 5 (5) times in total, then work to end of row, at the same time picking up and working wrapped stitches according to description in the Knitting School. Work another 1 row where remaining wrapped stitches are picked up and worked.

Neckband

Knit 1 rnd and at the same time, decrease 3 (1) 3 (1) 1 (11) 13 (21) sts evenly spaced across the rnd = 82 (90) 94 (102) 114 (122) 126 (130) sts.

Change to circular needle 4.5 mm and cast off the 5 steek stitches at the front.

Work in rib back and forth:

Row 1 (RS): *k2, p2*, repeat from *-* to last 2 sts, k2.
Row 2 (WS): *p2, k2*. Repeat from *-* to last 2 sts, p2.

Repeat rows 1 and 2 until the rib measures 4 cm. Finish with a wrong-side row.

Dec row: *k2, p2tog*. Repeat from *-* to last 2 sts, k2 = 62 (68) 71 (77) 86 (92) 95 (98) sts. Cast off loosely in rib.

Join sleeves to body at underarm

With 3.5 mm dpns: Knit the stitches from the body and the sleeves together using the 3-needle cast off method (see Knitting School, page 164). Weave in loose ends.

Button bands

LEFT BUTTON BAND

With circular needle 4.5 mm and colour 2 (RS): Pick up stitches along the left front edge starting from the top. To make the edge flexible, pick up from 2 of 3 rows of the front edge (= *pick up 2 sts, skip the den 3rd st*, repeat from *-*). The number of stitches must be divisible by 4 + 2.

Now work in rib stitch:

Row 1 (WS): *p2, k2*, repeat from *-* to last 2 sts, p2.

Row 2 (RS): *k2, p2*, repeat from *–* to last 2 sts, k2.
Row 3 (WS): *p2, k2*, repeat from *–* to last 2 sts, p2.

Repeat rows 2 and 3, four times in total (= 9 rows in total). Cast off in rib.

RIGHT BUTTON BAND

With 4.5 mm circular needle and colour 2 (RS): Pick up stitches along the right front edge starting from the bottom. Make sure to pick up the same number of stitches as on left button band. Distribute 5 or 9 buttonholes evenly across the edge, depending how dense you want them and indicate with markers on the needle. (Each buttonhole goes over 2 sts.)

Work in rib according to instructions for left side up to and including row 3.

Row 4 (buttonhole row 1, RS): Work in established rib to the first buttonhole then work as follows: *Cast off 2 sts, continue in established rib pattern to the next buttonhole*. Repeat from *–* until you have completed all buttonholes and thereafter work in rib to end of row.

Row 5 (buttonhole row 2, AS): Work in rib to the first buttonhole and finish as follows: *Cast on 2 sts using the double twisted loop technique, continue in rib pattern to the next buttonhole*. Repeat from *–* until all buttonholes have been finished and then work in rib to end of row.

Work another 4 rows in rib and then cast off in rib.

Cutting the steek

See Knitting School, page 160. Sew a reinforcing seam with sewing thread (by hand using backstitch) on each side of the middle steek stitch. Carefully cut the cardigan open in the middle of the middle steek stitch. (The cut edges will roll in towards the wrong side.)

Finishing

Weave in loose ends. Block the cardigan carefully according to the instructions in the Knitting School, page 161. Sew on buttons to correspond with the buttonholes. Either cover the cut edges on the inside with a decorative band, or fold them in and sew with discreet stitches to the wrong side (see Knitting School, pages 160–161).

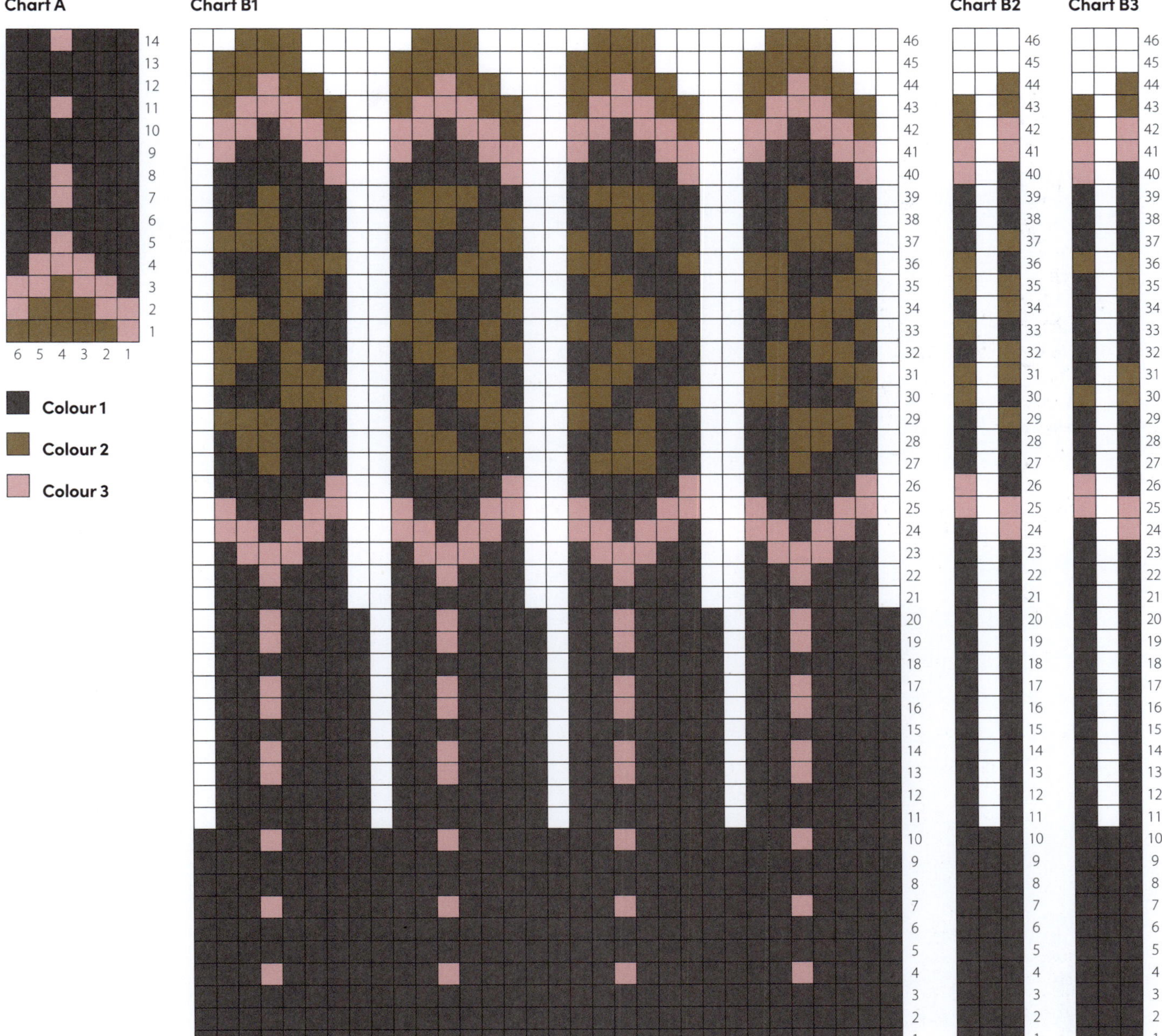
Chart A
Chart B1
Chart B2
Chart B3
Colour 1
Colour 2
Colour 3

Novel

AUTUMN

In libris libertas – in books, there is freedom! Wise words, don't you agree?

The whole world can fit inside a book. Through them we can move freely in time and space, experiencing things we have never experienced before and feeling what we have never felt. We get to try our wings, discover new perspectives and learn more about life – something I wanted to celebrate in this cardigan.

Novel is the perfect reading cardigan. Something to wear on a bleak autumn's day, when all you want to do is to sink deep into an armchair with your favourite book and a cup of warming tea. The classic tweed yarn gives a lively structure and ages beautifully thanks to its timeless charm. A little bit like a really good novel!

Yarn: Select no. 1 from Järbo (Mohair Tweed Yarn from Donegal, 70% merino, 30% mohair, 50 g = 110 m/120 yd)
Tension: 18 sts × 27 rows stocking stitch using 4.5 mm (US 7) needles = 10 × 10 cm
Sizes: XS (S) M (L) XL (2XL) 3XL (4XL)
Bust: 90 (98) 106 (114) 122 (130) 138 (146) cm/35½ (38½) 41¾ (45) 48 (51¼) 54¼ (57½) in
Length: 42 (44) 46 (48) 50 (52) 54 (56) cm/16½ (17¼) 18 (19) 19¾ (20½) 21¼ (22) in
Sleeve length: 44 (45) 45 (46) 46 (47) 47 (48) cm/ 17¼ (17¾) 17¾ (18) 18 (18½) 18½ (19) in
Amounts: 350 (350) 350 (400) 400 (450) 450 (500) g Brambleberry Jam (no. 22314)
Circular needles: 4 mm (US 6) and 4.5 mm (US 7), 80 cm
Double-pointed needles: 4 mm (UK 8/US 6) and 4.5 mm (US 7)
Notions: 5 buttons (approx. 20 mm in diameter), 4 stitch markers, stitch holder
Difficulty level: 2 of 3
Construction: The cardigan is knitted back and forth, from the top down with an integrated button band made up of garter stitch and i-cord edge.
Techniques: N.B. The button band runs over 9 sts at each side of the work.
BUTTON BAND (RS) = Slip the 2 first stitches purlwise with yarn at back of work, k5. Slip 1 st purlwise with yarn at back of work, p1. When 9 sts remain on the row: p1, slip 1 st purlwise, k5, k2.
BUTTON BAND (WS) = Slip the 2 first stitches purlwise with yarn at front of work, k5, p1, k1. When 9 sts remain: k1, p1, k5, p2.
BUTTONHOLE ROW 1 (RS) = Slip the 2 first stitches purlwise with yarn at back of work, k5. Slip 1 st purlwise with yarn at back of work, p1, knit to last 9 sts on the row, p1. Slip 1 st purlwise with yarn at back of work, k1, k2tog, yo, k4.
BUTTONHOLE ROW 2 (WS) = Slip 2 sts purlwise with yarn at front of work, k5, p1, k1. Purl to last 9 sts on the row, k1, p1, k5, k2.
SM = slip marker, see Knitting School, page 163.

Yoke

RIBBED NECKBAND

With 4 mm circular needle: Cast on 107 (111) 111 (113) 113 (115) 115 (117) sts.

Row 1 (WS): p2, k5, *p1, k1*. Repeat from *–* to last 8 sts on the row, p1, k5, p2.

Row 2 (RS): Work 9 sts of button band (see Techniques), k1, *p1, k1*. Repeat from *–* to last 9 sts on the row, work button band.

Row 3 (WS): Work 9 sts of button band, p1, *k1, p1*. Repeat from *–* to last 9 sts on the row, work button band.

Repeat rows 2 and 3 until the work measures 2.5 cm. N.B. Finish with a wrong-side row.

Make a buttonhole by working buttonhole row 1 and 2 (see Techniques). On buttonhole row 2, raglan stitch markers are placed (read about stitch markers on page 163 in the Knitting School) according to the following: raglan marker D after 24 (25) 25 (26) 26 (27) 27 (28) sts; raglan marker C after 12 (12) 12 (11) 11 (10) 10 (9) sts; raglan marker B after 35 (37) 37 (39) 39 (41) 41 (43) sts; raglan marker A after 12 (12) 12 (11) 11 (10) 10 (9) sts. N.B. Another 4 buttonholes are made every 9 (9.5) 10 (10.5) 11 (11.5) 12 (12.5) cm.

RAGLAN INCREASES AND SHORT ROWS

N.B. Remember to pick up and knit the wrapped stitches when you pass them. Read more about this and short rows on page 162.

Short row 1 (RS): Change to 4.5 mm circular needle and work 9 sts of button band. *Knit to last 1 st before raglan marker, M1R (see Knitting School, page 163), k1, SM (see Techniques), k1, M1L* (see Knitting School, page 163). Repeat from *–* another 3 times, wrap and turn = 8 new stitches.

Short row 2 (WS): Purl to raglan marker A, p3, wrap and turn.

Short row 3: Make raglan increases as in row 1. Knit to previous turn: knit another 3 sts, wrap and turn.

Short row 4: Purl to previous turn, purl another 3 sts, wrap and turn.

Repeat rows 3 and 4 another 1 (1) 1 (2) 2 (2) 3 (3) times.

Last short row: Knit to end of row with raglan increases and 9 sts of button band at the end.

Continue in stocking stitch (= knit on the right side and purl on the wrong side), make raglan increases on all knit rows and button bands according to pattern as set until you have a total of 299 (327) 343 (353) 369 (387) 403 (421) sts on the needle. Finish with a wrong-side row.

Divide for body and sleeves

Next row (RS): Work 9 sts of button band, k48 (52) 54 (56) 58 (61) 63 (66) to stitch marker A, remove marker and place the following 60 (66) 70 (71) 75 (78) 82 (85) sleeve stitches on a stitch holder/scrap yarn. Remove marker B, cast on 0 (0) 4 (8) 12 (14) 18 (20) new stitches for underarm using the double twisted loop technique (see video links in the Knitting School, page 164). K83 (91) 95 (99) 103 (109) 113 (119), remove marker C, place the following 60 (66) 70 (71) 75 (78) 82 (85) sleeve stitches on a stitch holder. Remove marker D, cast on 0 (0) 4 (8) 12 (14) 18 (20) new stitches for underarm using the double twisted loop technique, k39 (43) 45 (47) 49 (52) 54 (57) to last 9 sts on the row, work button band. Now you should have 179 (195) 211 (227) 243 (259) 275 (291) sts for the body on the needle.

Body

Continue working in stocking stitch, with button bands and buttonholes in established pattern until the body measures 22 (23) 24 (25) 26 (27) 28 (29) cm from the armhole. Finish with a wrong-side row.

BOTTOM RIB

Change to 4 mm circular needle.

Row 1 (RS): Work 9 sts of button band, k1, *p1, k1*. Repeat from *–* to last 9 sts on the row, work button band.

Row 2: Work 9 sts of button band, p1, *k1, p1*. Repeat from *–* to last 9 sts on the row, work button band.

Repeat rows 1 and 2 until the rib measures 3 cm, ending with a WS row. Cast off the button bands knitwise and the rest of the row in rib.

Sleeves

With 4.5 mm dpns: Divide the 60 (66) 70 (71) 75 (78) 82 (85) sleeve stitches over the needles. Pick up and place on dpns 0 (0) 2 (3) 5 (7) 9 (10) new stitches starting from centre of the armhole, knit 60 (66) 70 (71) 75 (78) 82 (85) sts of sleeve, then pick up another 0 (0) 2 (3) 5 (7) 9 (10) sts from the armhole to the centre = 60 (66) 74 (77) 85 (92) 100 (105) sts. Place a stitch marker at the start of the row and knit in the round in stocking stitch (= knit all rows when knitting in the round).

Knit until the sleeve measures 1 cm from the armhole.

Dec rnd: k1, slip 1 st, k1 and pass the slipped stitch over. Knit to last 3 sts on the rnd, k2tog, k1.

Repeat the decrease rnd after 4.5 (4) 4 (3.5) 3 (2.5) 2.5 (2) cm 6 (7) 8 (9) 11 (12) 13 (15) times = 46 (50) 56 (57) 63 (66) 72 (73) sts.

Knit until the sleeve measures 36 (37) 37 (38) 38 (39) 39 (40) cm from the armhole.

Decrease 6 (10) 14 (13) 17 (20) 26 (25) sts evenly spaced over the last rnd = 40 (40) 42 (44) 44 (46) 46 (48) sts.

Change to 4 mm dpns and work in rib (k1, p1) for 8 cm. Cast off loosely in rib.

Make a second sleeve the same way.

Finishing

Weave in loose ends. Block the cardigan carefully according to the instructions in the Knitting School, page 161. Sew on buttons to correspond with the buttonholes.

N CAR SA

Legacy

AUTUMN

The cardigan Legacy means a lot to me. This is because it's my version of a cardigan that my grandfather Allan brought home with him from Rjukan in Norway where he grew up. The original cardigan has been worn and loved by many in the family – first by my dad and then by me. It is probably from the 1940s, but it is still in good condition despite wear and age.

I am not the first to knit my own version of this cardigan – according to my dad my grandmother Elsa also made one in linden flower green. I want to do the same as soon as I can to keep the legacy alive!

Throughout the years I have often been asked about the pattern from interested knitters. Now I have finally made a reconstruction, so that this beautiful cardigan can get a new lease of life. I have been true to the original when it comes to the actual construction – the cardigan is knitted in the round the Norwegian way and is cut open at the front and at the armholes. Some details have been adjusted however – such as the button bands and the neckband. I hope you will enjoy it as much as I have.

Yarn: Sisu from Sandnes (80% wool, 20% nylon, 50 g = 175 m/191 yd)
Tension: 27 sts × 28 rows in stocking stitch in pattern using 3 mm (US 2.5) needles = 10 × 10 cm
Sizes: S (M/L) XL (2XL)
Bust: 91 (102) 113 (124) cm/35¾ (40¼) 44½ (48¾) in
Length: 60 (62) 64 (66) cm/23½ (24½) 25¼ (26) in
Sleeve length: 52 (53) 54 (55) cm/20½ (20¾) 21¼ (21¾) in
Amounts: Colour 1 = 450 (550) 600 (700) g Svart (no. 1099)
Colour 2 = 100 (100) 150 (150) g Hvit (no. 1002)
Colour 3 = 50 (50) 50 (50) g Rød (no. 4219)
Double-pointed needles: 2.5 mm (US 1.5) and 3 mm (US 2.5)
Circular needles: 2.5 mm (US 1.5) and 3 mm (US 2.5), 80 cm
Notions: 8 buttons (15 mm in diameter), stitch holder
Difficulty level: 3 of 3
Construction: The body is knitted in the round, from the bottom up, then the cardigan is cut open at the front (see Knitting School, page 160) – and at the armholes, the Norwegian way. The sleeves are knitted separately and then sewn onto the body. Then button bands and neckband are knitted on.
Techniques: M1b = increase 1 st in the stich below, see Knitting School, page 163.
M1R = increase 1 st slanting right, see Knitting School, page 163.
M1L = increase 1 st slanting left, see Knitting School, page 163.

Body

With circular needle 2.5 mm and colour 1: Cast on 267 (297) 327 (357) sts. Work in rib back and forth:

Row 1 (WS): p1, *k1, p1*, repeat from *–* to end of row.
Row 2: (RS): k1, *p1, k1*, repeat from *–* to end of row.
Row 3: p1, *k1, p1*, repeat from *–* to end of row.

Repeat rows 2 and 3 until the work measures 2 cm. Finish with a wrong-side row.

BUTTONHOLES

Buttonhole row 1: Work 6 sts in rib as set, cast off 3 sts, work in rib to end of row.

Buttonhole row 2: Work in rib as set until you reach the cast off stitches, cast on 3 new stitches using the double twisted loop technique (see video links in Knitting School, page 164). Work in rib to end of row.

Continue working in rib until the work measures 6 cm. Finish with a wrong-side row.

PREPARE FOR KNITTING IN THE ROUND

Work 13 sts in rib, then place these 13 sts as well as the corresponding 13 sts at the end of the row on a stitch holder/scrap yarn.

Change to 3 mm circular needle and knit to end of row (don't knit the stitches on the stich holders), then cast on 5 steek stitches using the double twisted loop technique. The steek stitches also work as a 'marker' for the beginning and end of a rnd. (N.B. The steek stitches don't count towards the cardigan's total stitch count, and any increases or decreases should not be made within these stitches.)

Continue in stocking stitch until the work measures 37 (39) 41 (43) cm. (Approx. 23 cm remains to full length.)

BODY, CONTINUED

Work the colour pattern according to chart A, rnd 1–18.

Place the chart according to size:

S: Repeat stitches 1–20 to last 1 stitch, then finish with stitch 1 in the chart.

M/L: Knit stitches 16–20, then repeat stitches 1–20 to last 6 stitches, then knit stitches 1–6.

XL: Repeat stitches 1–20 to last 1 stitch, then finish with stitch 1 in the chart.

2XL: Repeat stitches 1–20 to last 1 stitch then finish with stitch 1 in the chart. Then knit the pattern according to chart B, rows 1–46.

Place the chart according to size:

S: Knit stitches 24, then repeat stitches 1–24 to last 1 stitch, then finish with stitch 1 in the chart.

M/L: Knit stitches 22–24, then repeat stitches 1–24 to last 4 stitches, then knit stitches 1–4.

XL: Knit stitches 19–24, then repeat stitches 1–24 to last 7 stitches, then knit stitches 1–7.

2XL: Knit stitches 16–24, then repeat stitches 1–24 to last 10 stitches, then stitches 1–10.

AT THE SAME TIME – shape neck.

When you are 7 cm away from full length, the neckline is formed. (Now you have knitted approx. 16 cm of the colourwork.) Shape front neck as follows:

Cast off the 5 steek stitches and place the 9 (7) 11 (9) sts on each side of the steek stitches on a stitch holder.

(The rest of the chart is knitted back and forth in stocking stitch.) Next; cast off start of every neck edge row as follows: 4 sts at beg next neck row; 2 sts at beg next 2 neck rows; 1 sts at beg next 3 neck rows.

After casting off for the neckline the chart is completed. (Now the work should measure approx. 59 (61) 63 (65) cm.)

Next row is a RS row with sts cast off to mark the steek stitches at the sides:

With colour 2: k40 (48) 53 (61) (= shoulder stitches), Cast off 1 st (= steek stitch for armhole), k40 (48) 53 (61) (= shoulder stitches), k39 (41) 43 (45) (= neckline), k40 (48) 53 (61) (= shoulder stitches), Cast off 1 st (= steek stitch for armhole), k40 (48) 53 (61) (= shoulder stitches). Place the remaining stitches on a stitch holder.

Sleeves

With 2.5 mm dpns and colour 1: Cast on 52 sts.

Work in rib in the rnd (k1, p1) for 5 cm. Change to 3 mm dpns and place marker for beg of rnd.

Increase rnd 1: *k1, M1b (see Techniques), k1*. Repeat from *–* to end of rnd = 78 sts.

Continue in stocking stitch (= knit all rows when knitting in the round).

When the work measures 6 cm, start increases.

Increase rnd 2: *k1, M1L (see Techniques), knit to last 1 stitch on the row, M1R (see Techniques), k1.* Repeat from *–* after 1.5 cm 21 times = 120 sts.

Knit until the sleeve measures 39 (40) 41 (42) cm or 14 cm shorter than required length.

Knit the pattern according to chart C, Row 1–40. (Repeat sts 1–24 to end of row.)

After the chart: Turn the work and change direction of knitting – and knit another 7 rnds in stocking stitch with colour

2, which when assembling the cardigan is sewn so that the cut edge on the inside is covered.

Make a second sleeve the same way.

Cutting the steek

See instructions in the Knitting School, page 160. Sew reinforcing seams and carefully cut the steek at the middle.

Assembly

SEW AND CUT ARMHOLES OPEN

Sew reinforcing seams on each side of the side stitch where the armhole is cut open. The armhole should be 23 cm deep from the shoulder, corresponding to the depth of the colourwork section on the body (see photos). Start at the top by the shoulder and sew downwards to the stated length, then up to the shoulder again. Sew the seams in the middle of the stitches on each side of the side stitch. Carefully cut in-between the seams and make sure not to cut further than to the seam at the bottom of the armhole.

SEW SHOULDERS TOGETHER

Sew the shoulder stitches together using kitchener stitch (see Knitting School, page 164) and colour 3, so that you get a red stripe on the middle of the shoulder.

SEW ON THE SLEEVES

Make sure that the middle of the top of the sleeve aligns with the middle of the shoulder seam and that the beg of the round starting is in the centre of the underarm. Sew with kitchener stitch from the right side: on the sleeve, insert the needle in the transition between the chart and the interfacing, and on the body, the stitches are made by inserting the needle a whole stitch inside the seams on each side of the armhole. Turn the work with the wrong side facing out, place the interfacing over the cut edge and carefully sew it in place.

LEFT BUTTON BAND

Place the 13 sts from bottom rib that are held on the stitch holder on one of the 2.5 mm dpns.

Row 1 (RS): With colour 1: k1, *p1, k1*, repeat from *–* to end of row.

Row 2 (WS): p1, *k1, p1*, repeat from *–* to end of row. Then, cast on 4 new stitches using the double twisted loop technique. (These 4 sts make an interfacing that is then covering the cut edge on the inside.)

Row 3: p4, work in rib in pattern as set.

Row 4: Work in rib to last 4 sts, k4.

Repeat rows 3 and 4 until the button band reaches the first cast off that was made for the neckline. N.B. Keep in mind to stretch the edge slightly when measuring to make sure the button band becomes flexible.

Cast off the 4 interfacing stitches. Place remaining stitches on a stitch holder.

Mark the placements of the 8 buttons, using dressmaker pins for example. They should be spaced evenly over the edge, with the top button 1 cm in on the neckband, which is knitted last.

RIGHT BUTTON BAND

N.B. On the right-hand side the buttonholes are knitted according to the instruction at the beginning of the pattern, with corresponding placement to the markers for the buttons on the left-hand side.

Place the 13 sts from the stitch holder on 2.5 mm dpns.

Row 1 (WS): With colour 1: p1, *k1, p1*, repeat from *–* to end of row.

Row 2 (RS): k1, *p1, k1*, repeat from *–* to end of row, then cast on 4 new stitches using the double twisted loop technique. (These 4 sts make an interfacing that is then covering the cut edge on the inside.)
Row 3: k4, work in rib in established pattern.
Row 4: Work in rib in established pattern to last 4 sts, p4.

Repeat rows 3 and 4 until the button band reaches the first cast off that was made for the neckline. N.B. Keep in mind to stretch the edge slightly when measuring to make sure the button band gets flexible.

Cast off the 4 interfacing stitches. Place the remaining stitches on a stitch holder.

Carefully sew the edges and the interfacing over the cut edges.

NECKBAND

With 2.5 mm circular needle and colour 1: Place the 13 sts from the button band that are on the stitch holder on the needle and rib them. Then pick up stitches evenly around the neck edge and rib the 13 sts from the other stitch holder so that you get 135 (135) 141 (141) sts in total.
Row 1 (WS): p1, *k1, p1*, repeat from *–* to end of row.
Row 2: (RS): k1, *p1, k1*, repeat from *–* to end of row.
Row 3: p1, *k1, p1*, repeat from *–* to end of row.

Repeat rows 2 and 3 until the edge measures 1 cm. Finish with a wrong-side row.

Make a buttonhole as before.

Work in rib until the edge measures 3 cm.

On the following 2 rows the 13 stitches at each end are cast off. Work in rib another 3 cm. Cast off loosely in rib. Fold the edge double towards the inside and sew it in place with small stitches.

Finishing

Weave in loose ends. Block the cardigan carefully according to the instructions in the Knitting School, page 161. Sew on buttons to correspond with the buttonholes.

Chart A

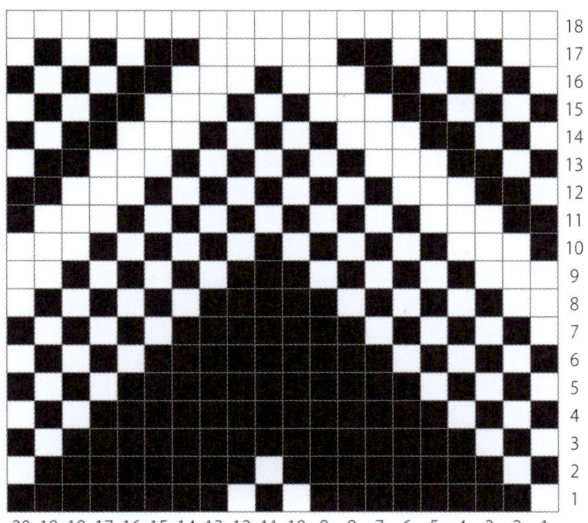

Chart C

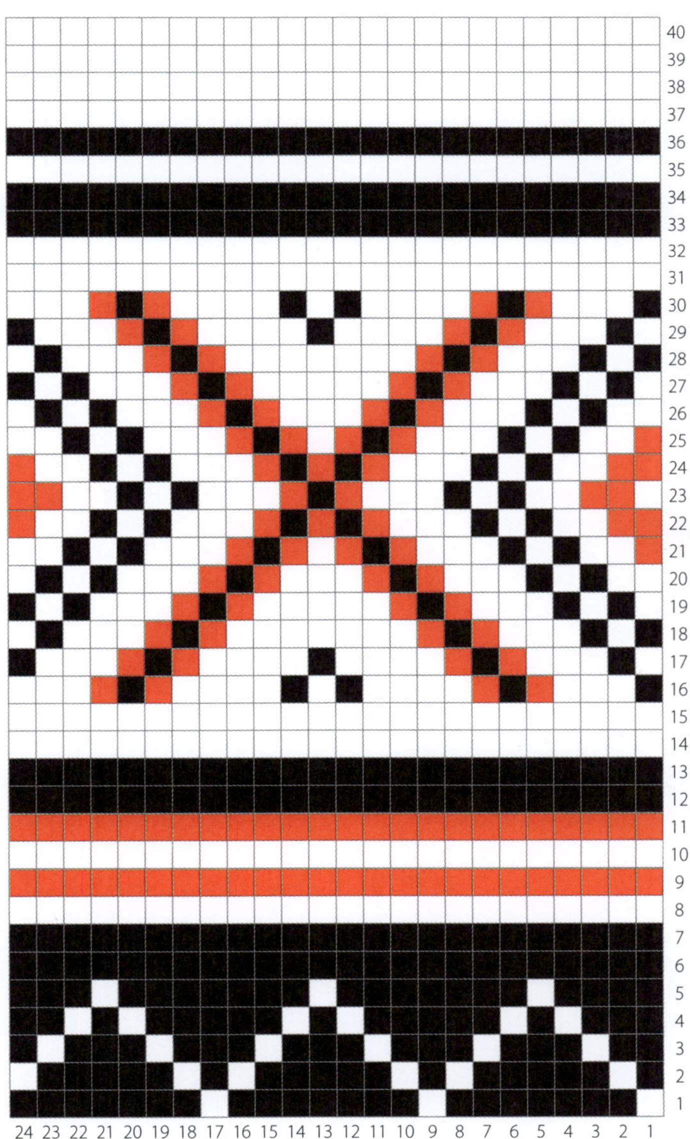

Chart B

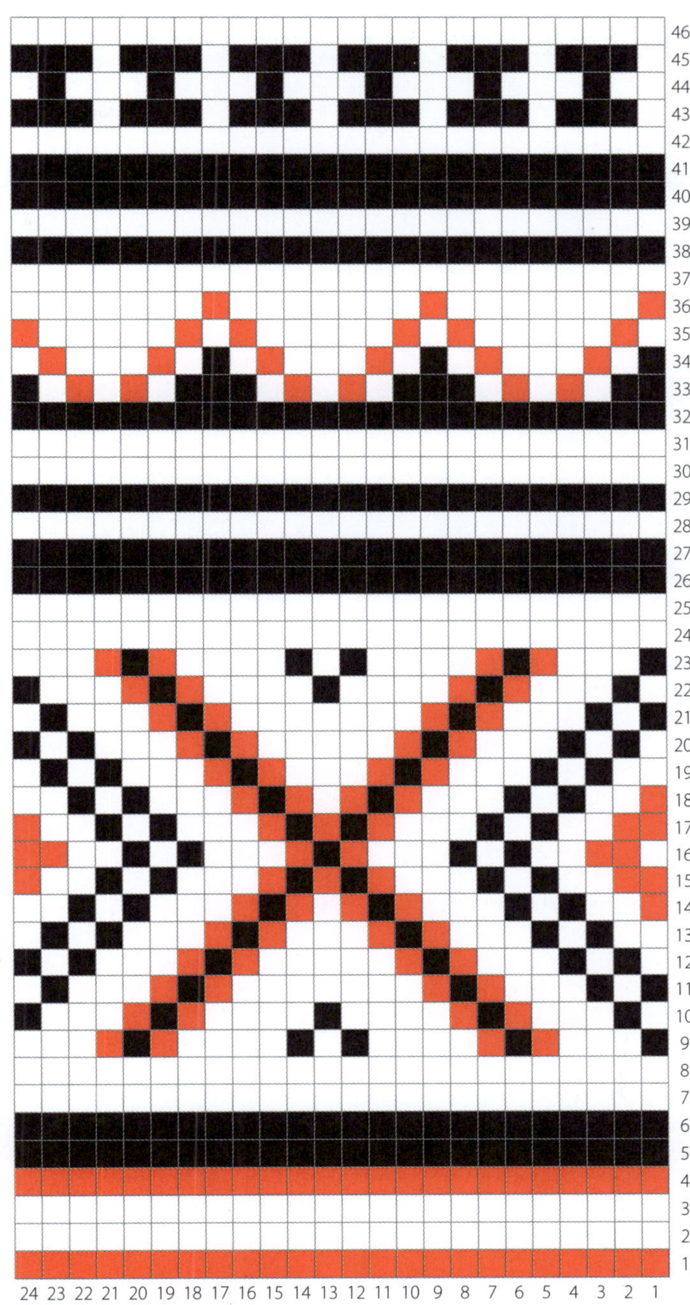

Colour 1

Colour 2

Colour 3

Sisterhood

AUTUMN

The dancing sisters are back, this time in the form of a cardigan – if you have knitted my mittens and socks before you might recognize them.

There is something beautiful about using the traditional Swedish ring dance as a symbol for how we help each other forwards in life, generation after generation. The ring dance is like an infinite circle of care. One moment you are a little girl holding your mother's hand, and then, before you know it, you're standing there yourself: as a mother, grandmother or perhaps even as a great-grandmother. The circle of life is full of wonder. But love ties us together so we are all united – even beyond time and space. The Sisterhood cardigan is a fine-knit wool cardigan full of warmth!

Yarn: Järbo 2-ply wool (100% wool, approx. 100 g = 300 m/327 yd)
Tension: 25 sts × 30 rows in stocking stitch in pattern using 3 mm (US 2.5) needles = 10 × 10 cm
Sizes: XS (S) M (L) XL (2XL) 3XL
Bust: 87 (96) 105 (115) 125 (134) 143 cm/34$\frac{1}{4}$ (37$\frac{3}{4}$) 41$\frac{1}{4}$ (45$\frac{1}{4}$) 49$\frac{1}{4}$ (52$\frac{3}{4}$) 56$\frac{1}{4}$ in
Length: 42 (43) 45 (46) 48 (51) 53 cm/16$\frac{1}{2}$ (17) 17$\frac{3}{4}$ (18) 19 (20) 20$\frac{3}{4}$ in
Sleeve length: 48 (49) 50 (50) 50 (53) (53) cm/ 19 (19$\frac{1}{4}$) 19$\frac{3}{4}$ (19$\frac{3}{4}$) 19$\frac{3}{4}$ (20$\frac{3}{4}$) 20$\frac{3}{4}$ in
Amounts: Colour 1 = 300 (300) 300 (400) 450 (450) (500) g Blackish (no. 74109)
Colour 2 = 100 (100) 100 (150) 150 (150) (200) g Natural White (no. 74102)
Circular needles: 3 mm (US 2.5), 80 cm
Double-pointed needles: 2.5 mm (US 1.5) and 3 mm (US 2.5)
Notions: 5 stitch markers, stitch holder
Other: 11 buttons (10 mm in diameter), decorative band (optional), approx. 1 m
Difficulty level: 3 of 3
Construction: The cardigan is knitted in the round from the bottom and up, body and sleeves are knitted separately and then joined at the yoke. To finish, the cardigan is cut open (see Knitting School, page 160) after the button bands are knitted on. The body is decorated with a wide patterned section at the bottom, which is edged with Latvian braids (see Knitting School, page 164). Other parts of the cardigan are decorated with lice stitches.
Techniques: M1L = increase 1 st slanting left, see Knitting School, page 163.
M1R = increase 1 st slanting right, see Knitting School, page 163.
Raglan decreases = knit to last 3 sts before raglan marker, slip 1 st, k1 and pass the slipped stitch over the knitted stitch. K1, slip marker from the left to the right needle, k1, k2tog. Repeat at all raglan stitch markers.

Body

With circular needle 3 mm and colour 1: Cast on 217 (241) 265 (289) 313 (337) 361 sts. In addition to these stitches, cast on 5 steek stitches. The steek stitches also work as a 'marker' for the beginning and end of a row. (N.B. The steek stitches don't count towards the cardigan's total stitch count, and any increases or decreases should not be made within these stitches.)

Join to knit in the round and start with Latvian braid (see Knitting School, page 164). N.B. The 5 steek stitches are knitted in stocking stitch, not in Latvian braid.

Rnd 1: *k1 with colour 1, k1 with colour 2*. Repeat from *-* to last 1 st, k1 with colour 1.

Rnd 2: *p1 with colour 1, p1 with colour 2*. Repeat from *-* to last 1 st, p1 with colour 1. N.B. Hold both threads at the front of the work when knitting. For each colour change the new yarn should go under the yarn you just knitted with.

Rnd 3: *p1 with colour 1, p1 with colour 2*. Repeat from *-* to last 1 st, p1 with colour 1. N.B. Hold both threads at the front of the work when knitting. For each colour change the new yarn should go over the yarn you just knitted with.

Change to stocking stitch (= knit all rnds when knitting in the round) and knit 2 rnds with colour 1.

Knit the pattern according to chart A, rnds 1–21 (stitches 1–12 are repeated to last 1 st on the rnd, then knit stitch 1 in the chart).

With colour 1: Knit 2 rnds.

Make another Latvian braid according to the instructions above. From now on the body is knitted in stocking stitch (= knit all rows when knitting in the round).

With colour 1: Knit 3 rnds.

Knit the pattern according to chart B, rnds 1–8 (stitches 1–4 are repeated to last 1 st, then knit st 1 in the chart). Repeat rnds 1–8 until the work measures 26 (26) 27 (28) 30 (32) 34 cm or length of your choice. N.B. Finish on rnd 4 or 8 in the chart.

ARMHOLES

Cast off as follows: Knit 50 (55) 60 (65) 70 (75) 80 sts (= right front), cast off 9 (11) 13 (15) 17 (19) 21 st (after casting off 1 st remains on the right needle). Knit 98 (108) 118 (128) 138 (148) 158 sts (= back) Cast off 9 (11) 13 (15) 17 (19) 21 st (after casting off 1 st remains on the right needle), knit 49 (54) 59 (64) 69 (74) 79 sts (= left front) = 198 (218) 238 (258) 278 (298) 318 sts.

Place the stitches from the body on a stitch holder/scrap yarn and set the work aside.

Right sleeve

With 2.5 mm dpns and colour 1: Cast on 56 (56) 60 (60) 68 (68) 68 sts.

Work rib stitch in the round (k1, p1) for 5 cm.

From now on the sleeve is worked in stocking stitch (= knit all rnds when knitting in the round).

Change to 3 mm dpns and knit 2 rnds. N.B. Place a stitch marker on the needle to mark the start of the rnd, this will make it easier to control that the pattern is placed evenly.

Work the pattern according to chart B, rnds 1–8 (stitches 1–4 are repeated to end of row).

Repeat chart B, rnds 1–8 another 1 time.

Now begin increases at the same time as continuing pattern according to chart B. As new stitches are added with the increases, these should be incorporated into the lice stitch pattern. The chart isn't evenly divisible across all rows, it's

therefore important to keep the stitch marker in place as the starting point and let the pattern increase either side.

Inc row: k1, M1L (see Techniques), Knit to last 1 st on the row, M1R (see Techniques), k1.

Continue working the pattern in stocking stitch and repeat the increase row every 2.5 (2.5) 2.5 (2) 2 (2) 2 cm, until there are 82 (86) 90 (96) 100 (106) 110 sts on the needle.

Knit until the sleeve measures approx. 48 (49) 50 (50) 50 (53) 53 cm but adjust the length according to the pattern knitting. N.B. Finish on row 3 or 7 in the chart so that the following row corresponds with the next row of the body (= row 4 or row 8 in the chart).

Cast off the sleeve underarm as follows: Cast off 4 (5) 6 (7) 8 (9) 10 sts, knit to last 5 (6) 7 (8) 9 (10) 11 st on the row, cast off 5 (6) 7 (8) 9 (10) 11 sts = 73 (75) 77 (81) 83 (87) 89 sts on the needle.

Place the sleeve stitches on a stitch holder and set the work aside.

Left sleeve

Is knitted as the right sleeve, but pattern chart B should be mirrored so the sleeve matches the front.

Yoke

Now all the parts are knitted together.

With circular needle 3 mm, colour 1 and right side facing; place the parts on the circular needle as follows:

Right front: 50 (55) 60 (65) 70 (75) 80 sts.
Right sleeve: 73 (75) 77 (81) 83 (87) 89 sts.
Back: 99 (109) 119 (129) 139 (149) 159.
Left sleeve: 73 (75) 77 (81) 83 (87) 89 sts.
Left front: 50 (55) 60 (65) 70 (75) 80 sts.

Now you should have 345 (369) 393 (421) 445 (473) 497 sts on the needle.

Knit 1 rnd at the same time as you place stitch markers as follows:

1 marker at beginning of rnd, 1 raglan marker between right front and right sleeve, 1 raglan marker between right sleeve and back panel.

1 raglan marker between back panel and left sleeve and 1 raglan marker between left sleeve and left front. You should have placed 4 raglan markers in total, and 1 marker at the beginning of the rnd.

Continue knitting lice stitch pattern according to chart B, with the same placement as before for each part respectively. However, work the 4 sts before and after each stitch marker in colour 1 (see photo) (see note about colourwork knitting in Knitting School).

RAGLAN DECREASES

Knit in stocking stitch and make raglan decreases (see Techniques) on each rnd 7 (8) 8 (9) 10 (12) 14 times in total. Then make raglan decreases on every other rnd 19 (21) 23 (24) 25 (23) 23 times in total = 137 (137) 145 (157) 165 (193) 201 sts.

NECK SHAPING

Knit to last 10 (10) 10 (11) 11 (12) 12 sts before the steek stitches and then cast off 20 (20) 20 (22) 22 (24) 24 sts as well as the 5 steek stitches in the middle – this way you form the neckline.

Continue with the rnd that was started with the cast off and make raglan decreases as before on this rnd. From here the remainder of the cardigan is knitted back and forth in stocking stitch – continue in lice stitch pattern as set.

Next (WS): Turn, p2tog, purl to end of row.

Continue in stocking stitch decreasing 1 st at the beginning of all rows for neck shaping as follows: On right side rows– slip 1, k1 and pass the slipped stitch over the knitted stitch.

On wrong side rows: p2tog at beg of rows.

AT THE SAME TIME, on right side rows, continue with raglan decreases, until 24 (26) 28 (29) 30 (30) 31 decreases have been made in total on every other row. (The 7 (8) 8 (9) 10 (12) 14 first raglan decreases are not included in this number.) N.B. The two last decrease rows are not knitted in pattern, only with colour 1. After the last row with raglan decrease, finish with a wrong side row as follows: p2tog, purl to last 2 sts on the needle, p2tog = 67 (67) 75 (85) 93 (99) 97 sts. Leave the stitches on hold.

Button bands

RIGHT BUTTON BAND (WITH BUTTONHOLES)

With right side facing: Pick up 116 (116) 118 (120) 124 (128) 132 sts along the right front edge starting from the bottom. N.B. Space the stitches evenly by skipping every 4th row when picking up the stitches (= *pick up 3 sts, skip the 4th st*, repeat from *–*).

Knit 3 rows.

Make the buttonholes:

XS: k2, * k2tog, yo, k9*. Repeat from *–* another 9 times, k2tog, yo, k2.

S: k2, * k2tog, yo, k9*. Repeat from *–* another 9 times, k2tog, yo, k2.

M: k3, * k2tog, yo, k9*. Repeat from *–* another 9 times, k2tog, yo, k3.

L: k4, * k2tog, yo, k9*. Repeat from *–* another 9 times, k2tog, yo, k4.

XL: k6, * k2tog, yo, k9*. Repeat from *–* another 9 times, k2tog, yo, k6.

2XL: k3, * k2tog, yo, k10*. Repeat from *–* another 9 times, k2tog, yo, k3.

3XL: k5, * k2tog, yo, k10*. Repeat from *–* another 9 times, k2tog, yo, k5.

Knit 3 rows.

To make a sturdy edge that doesn't stretch with use, every fourth stitch is decreased when casting off. Cast off as follows: *Cast off 3 sts, k2tog, cast off the stitch that was knitted together*. Repeat from *–* until all stitches have been cast off. (N.B. The cast off can be finished at any stage in the repeating sequence.)

LEFT BUTTON BAND

With right side facing: Pick up 116 (116) 118 (120) 124 (128) 132 sts along the left front edge starting from the top. Knit 7 rows.

Cast off the same way as for the right button band.

Neckband

With right side facing and starting at right button band: Pick up new stitches along the right neckline – 1 st in each of the following 3 sts, skip 1 st and repeat the same sequence until you reach the existing stitches held at the Back Neck. Knit the 67 (67) 75 (85) 93 (99) 97 sts and then pick up the same number of stitches as you picked up at the start of the row along the left neckline.

Knit 5 rows, back and forth. Cast off the same way as for the right button band.

Cutting the steek

See page 160 in the Knitting School. Sew a reinforcing seam with sewing thread (by hand using backstitch), on each side of the middle steek stitch. Carefully cut the cardigan open in the middle of the middle steek stitch. (The cut edges will roll in towards the wrong side.)

Finishing

Sew any gaps at the underarm using kitchener stitch. Weave in loose ends. Block the cardigan carefully according to the instructions in the Knitting School, page 161. Either cover the cut edges on the inside with a decorative band, or fold them in and sew with discreet stitches to the wrong side (see Knitting School, pages 160–161).

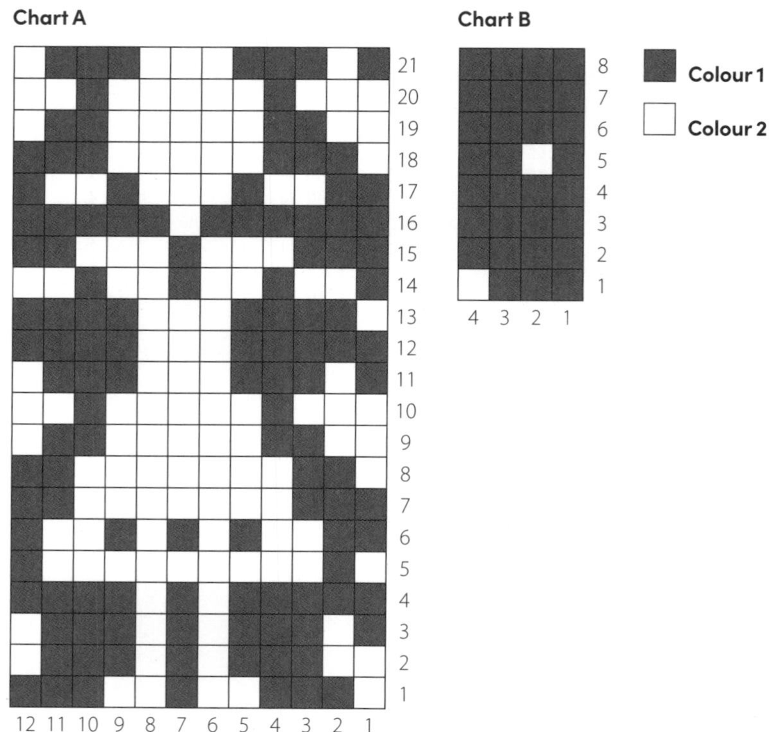
Chart A
Chart B
Colour 1
Colour 2

Leora

AUTUMN

The name Leora means 'my light' in Hebrew. There's also a Greek version of the name meaning 'compassion' or 'light'.

What I had in mind when making the Leora cardigan was those dark times when you long for the light to return, both literally and figuratively. Suddenly there is something that illuminates everything – a beacon of hope is lit and life feels lighter again. I hope that this cardigan can be just such a light for those who need it!

Thanks to its rustic and warming structure it will stand up to both autumn winds and rainstorms. The pattern's repetitive structure should also give you a bit of rest and recuperation while you knit it.

Yarn: Léttlopi from Ístex (100% Icelandic wool, 50 g = 100 m/109 yd)
Tension: 18 sts × 24 rows in stocking stitch in pattern using 5 mm (US 8) needles = 10 × 10 cm
Sizes: XS (S) M (L) XL (2XL) 3XL (4XL)
Bust: 85 (94) 98 (107) 120 (134) 143 (156) cm/ 33½ (37) 38½ (42¼) 47¼ (52¾) 56¼ (61½) in
Length: 47 (48.5) 51 (52) 55 (56.5) 58.5 (60 cm/18½ (19) 20 (20½) 21¾ (22¼) 23 (23½) in
Sleeve length: 44 (45) 47 (49) 51 (52) 52 (52) cm/17¼ (17¾) 18½ (19¼) 20 (20½) 20½ (20½) in
Amounts: Colour 1 = 350 (400) 450 (500) (500) 550 (600) (600) g Straw (no. 11418)
Colour 2 = 50 (100) 100 (100) 100 (150) 150 (150) g Air Blue (no. 11700)
Double-pointed needles: 4.5 mm (US 7) and 5 mm (US 8)
Circular needles: 4.5 mm (US 7) and 5 mm (US 8), 80 cm
Notions: 11 buttons (15 mm in diameter), stitch holder, decorative band (optional)
Difficulty level: 3 of 3
Construction: Body and sleeves are knitted in the round separately and are then placed together on one circular needle. Then the yoke is knitted with decreases, back short rows and a neckband. To finish, the cardigan is cut open (see Knitting School, page 160) after button bands are knitted on. Note that the rib at the bottom and top are knitted back and forth.
Techniques: M1L = increase 1 st slanting left, see Knitting School, page 163.
M1R = increase 1 st slanting right, see Knitting School, page 163.

Body

With 4.5 mm circular needle and colour 1: Cast on 146 (162) 174 (190) 214 (234) 250 (274) sts.

Work in rib back and forth:

Row 1 (WS): *p2, k2*, repeat from *-* to last 2 sts, p2.
Row 2 (RS): *k2, p2*, repeat from *-* to last 2 sts, k2.
Row 3 (WS): *p2, k2*, repeat from *-* to last 2 sts, p2.

Repeat rows 2 and 3 until the rib measures 5 cm. N.B. Finish the rib on a wrong side row.

From now on the body is knitted in the round in stocking stitch (= knit all rows when knitting in the round).

First row, with 5 mm needle: knit and at the same time increase 7 (7) 3 (3) 3 (7) 7 (7) sts evenly spaced across the rnd = 153 (169) 177 (193) 217 (241) 257 (281) sts.

Then, cast on 5 steek stitches using the double twisted loop technique (see video links in the Knitting School, page 164). The steek stitches also work as a 'marker' for the beginning and end of a rnd. (N.B. The steek stitches don't count towards the cardigan's total stitch count, and any increases or decreases should not be made within these stitches.)

Then knit another 1 rnd.

Work the pattern according to chart A, following the chart from right to left every row. Work rnds 1–37 with the following placement for each size, **XS:** knit stitches 1–24 six times in total, then stitches 1–9. (**S:** knit stitches 5–24, stitches 1–24 six times in total, then stitches 1–5.) **M:** knit stitches 1–24 seven times in total, then stitches 1–9. (**L:** knit stitches 5–24, stitches 1–24 seven times in total, then stitches 1–5.) **XL:** knit stitches 5–24, stitches 1–24 eight times in total, then stitches 1–5. (**2XL:** knit stitches 5–24, stitches 1–24 nine times in total, then stitches 1–5.) **3XL:** knit stitches 21–24, stitches 1–24 ten times in total, then stitches 1–13. (**4XL:** knit stitches 21–24, stitches 1–24 eleven times in total, then stitches 1–13.) With colour 1: Continue knitting until the body measures 25 (26) 27 (28) 29 (30) 31 (32) cm, or length of your choice. Set the work aside.

Sleeves

With 4.5 mm dpns and colour 1: Cast on 40 (40) 40 (40) 40 (44) 44 (44) sts.

Work rib stitch in the round (k2, p2) for 5 cm.

Change to 5 mm dpns and continue in stocking stitch (= knit all rows when knitting in the round), at the same time increase 8 (8) 8 (8) 8 (4) 4 (4) sts evenly spaced across the row = 48 (48) 48 (48) 48 (48) 48 (48) sts. Place marker at beg of rnd.

Knit another 1 rnd.

Work the pattern according to chart B for 13 rnds (stitches 1–24 are repeated 2 times in total).

With colour 1: Knit 2 rnds.

Inc rnd: *k1, M1L (see Techniques), knit to last 1 stitch on the rnd, M1R (see Techniques), k1.

Knit 19 (13) 9 (7) 5 (3) 3 (3) rnds without increases.*

Repeat from *-* 2 (4) 6 (10) 14 (18) 21 (23) times in total = 52 (56) 60 (68) 76 (84) 90 (94) sts.

Knit until the sleeve measures 44 (45) 47 (49) 51 (52) 52 (52) cm, or length of your choice.

Next rnd: Knit to last 4 (5) 5 (6) 7 (7) 8 (8) sts on the rnd. Place the following 8 (10) 10 (12) 14 (14) 16 (16) sts on a stitch holder/scrap yarn (= armhole stitches). Cut the yarn, place the sleeve's remaining 44 (46) 50 (56) 62 (70) 74 (78) sts on a stitch holder. Set the work aside and make a second sleeve the same way.

Join body and sleeves

Continue knitting in the round in stocking stitch. With 5 mm circular needle and colour 1: Knit the right front 34 (37) 39 (42) 47 (53) 56 (62) sts. Place the following 8 (10) 10 (12) 14 (14) 16 (16) sts to a stitch holder. Knit the right sleeve 44 (46) 50 (56) 62 (70) 74 (78) sts. Knit the back panel 69 (75) 79 (85) 95 (107) 113 (125) sts. Place the following 8 (10) 10 (12) 14 (14) 16 (16) sts to a stitch holder. Knit left sleeve 44 (46) 50 (56) 62 (70) 74 (78) sts. Knit left front 34 (37) 39 (42) 47 (53) 56 (62) sts = 225 (241) 257 (281) 313 (353) 373 (405) sts on the needle.

Knit 1 rnd.

Next rnd, sizes **XS, S, M, 2XL:** knit. Sizes **L, XL, 3XL, 4XL:** Decrease 8 (8) 4 (4) sts evenly spaced = 225 (241) 257 (273) 305 (353) 369 (401) sts left on needle.

Yoke

Knit 11 (12) 13 (14) 16 (17) 18 (19) rnds.

Dec rnd 1: k1, *k6, k2tog*. Repeat from *–* to end of rnd = 197 (211) 225 (239) 267 (309) 323 (351) sts. Knit 8 rnds.

Dec rnd 2: k7, *k2tog, k12*. Repeat from *–* to last 8 sts on the rnd, k2tog, k6 = 183 (196) 209 (222) 248 (287) 300 (326) sts. Knit 11 rnds.

Dec rnd 3: k2, *k2tog, 1k1*. Repeat from *–* to last 1 st on the rnd, k1. Knit 2 rnds.

Dec rnd 4: k3, *k2tog, k4*. Repeat from *–* to last 4 sts on the rnd, k2tog, k2 = 141 (151) 161 (171) 191 (221) 231 (251) sts. Knit 5 rnds.

Dec rnd 5: k3, *k2tog, k3*. Repeat from *–* to last 3 sts on the rnd, k2tog, k1. Knit 2 rnds.

Dec rnd 6: k2, *k2tog, k2*. Repeat from *–* to last 3 sts on the rnd, k2tog, k1 = 85 (91) 97 (103) 115 (133) 139 (151) sts left on the needle.

Back short rows

Read about short rows and wrap and turn on page 162. From here work in stocking stitch back and forth with knit and purl short rows: Knit 56 (60) 64 (68) 76 (88) 92 (100) sts, wrap and turn. Purl 28 (30) 32 (34) 38 (44) 46 (50) sts, wrap and turn. *Knit to last 4 sts before the turn, wrap and turn. Purl to last 4 sts before the turn, wrap and turn.*

Repeat from *–* 2 (2) 3 (3) 4 (4) 5 (5) times in total, then knit to end of row and at the same time pick up the wrapped stitches and work them according to the instructions in the Knitting School. Lastly knit 1 row where the rest of the wrapped stitches are picked up and knitted.

Neckband

Knit 1 rnd and at the same time, decrease 3 (1) 3 (1) 1 (11) 13 (21) sts evenly spaced across the rnd = 82 (90) 94 (102) 114 (122) 126 (130) sts. Change to 4.5 mm circular needle and cast off the 5 steek stitches at the middle of the front.

Knit the neckband back and forth:

Row 1 (RS): *k2, p2*, repeat from *–* to last 2 sts, k2.

Row 2 (WS): *p2, k2*, repeat from *–* to last 2 sts, p2.

Repeat rows 1 and 2 until the neckband measures 4 cm. Finish with a wrong-side row.

Dec row: *k2, p2tog*. Repeat from *–* to last 2 sts, k2 = 62 (68) 71 (77) 86 (92) 95 (98) sts. Cast off loosely in rib.

Join sleeves to body at underarm

With 3.5 mm dpns: Knit together the stitches from the sleeves and the body underneath the armholes using the 3-needle cast off method (see Knitting School, page 164). Weave in loose ends.

Button bands

LEFT BUTTON BAND

With 4.5 mm circular needle and colour 1 (RS): Pick up stitches along the left front edge starting from the top. To make the edge flexible, pick up 2 of 3 sts (= *knit 2 sts, skip the 3rd st*, repeat from *–*). Make sure that the number of stitches that are picked up are divisible by 4 + 2 sts.

Now work in rib stitch:

Row 1 (WS): *p2, k2*, repeat from *–* to last 2 sts, p2.

Row 2 (RS): *k2, p2*, repeat from *–* to last 2 sts, k2.

Row 3 (WS): *p2, k2*, repeat from *–*to last 2 sts, p2.

Repeat rows 2 and 3 four times (= 9 rows in total). Cast off in rib.

RIGHT BUTTON BAND

With 4.5 mm circular needle and colour 1 (RS): Pick up stitches along the right front edge starting from the bottom. Make sure to pick up the same number of stitches as on the left side. Distribute 11 buttonholes evenly across the edge (each buttonhole goes over 2 sts) and place markers on needle.

Work in rib according to the description for the left button band to row 3.

Row 4 (buttonhole row 1, RS): Work in rib to the first buttonhole. Then work as follows: *Cast off 2 sts, continue in rib pattern as set to the next buttonhole*. Repeat from *–* until you have completed all buttonholes, then work in rib to end of row.

Row 5 (buttonhole row 2, WS): Work in rib to the first buttonhole and finish as follows: *Cast on 2 sts using the double twisted loop technique, continue in rib pattern to the next buttonhole*. Repeat from *–* until all buttonholes have been finished then work in rib to end of row.

Work another 4 rows in rib then cast off in rib.

Cutting the steek

See Knitting School, page 160. Sew a reinforcing seam with sewing thread (by hand using backstitch) on each side of the middle steek stitch. Carefully cut the cardigan open in the middle of the middle steek stitch. (The cut edges will roll in towards the wrong side.)

Finishing

Weave in loose ends. Block the cardigan carefully according to the instructions in the Knitting School, page 161. Sew on buttons to correspond with the buttonholes. Either cover the cut edges on the inside with a decorative band, or fold them in and sew with discreet stitches onto the wrong side (see Knitting School, pages 160–161).

Chart A

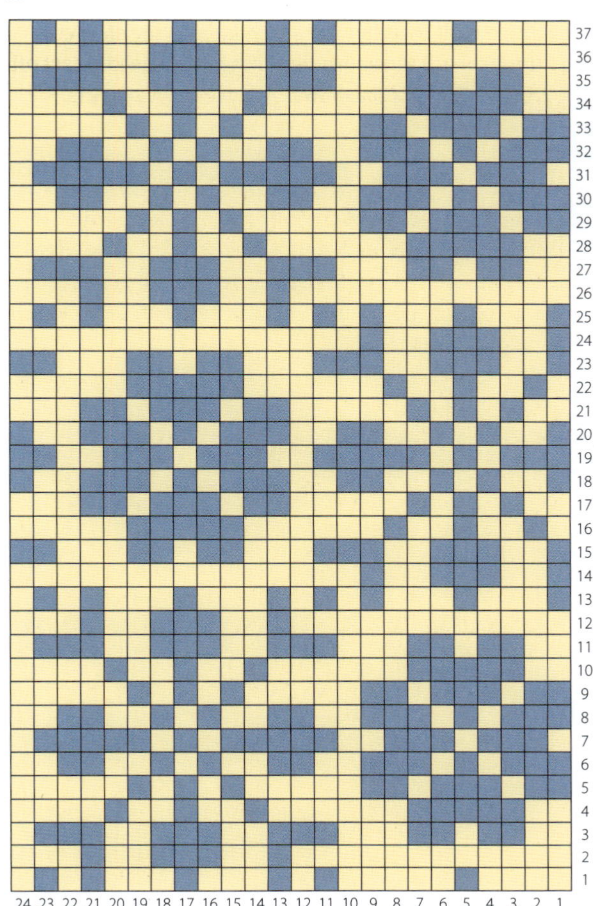

Chart B

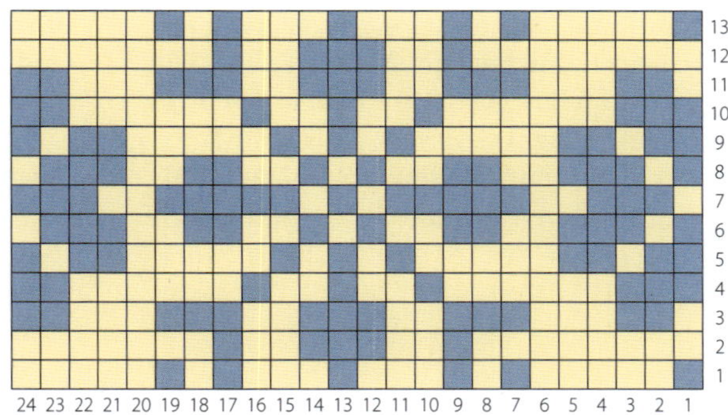

Colour 1

Colour 2

C. L.

In **winter**, calm envelops the country. Frozen lakes, vast landscapes and a silence that gives space for thoughtfulness – all of this provides a calming backdrop to the everyday routine.

At this time of the year, I just want to knit. Adding calm stitches in the light from the fire, adding log after log while listening to it crackle, I dive into the world of colourwork knitting. Around Christmas I usually cast on something extra special, a dream project that I have longed to do for a while. Then winter continues along its slow pace, punctuated with cardigan knitting, saffron buns and spruce wreaths.

One day we may go out on a skiing trip, dressed in wool from top to toe as we take the kicksled down to lake Billingen. We load the kicksled full of hot chocolate and sheepskins, and then we take a trip on the lake. The snow crunches under our feet and smoke rises from a chimney.

When I come back home, I cast on for a new cardigan. This is exactly what winter calls for.

Wreath

WINTER

A wreath has neither a beginning nor an end – its shape is infinite. It can symbolize honour and recognition, but also the sun's trajectory in the sky and eternal life. Perhaps you are making your own wreath to hang on the door during Advent. I have a soft spot for the classic evergreen, which also is the base for the yoke pattern on this cardigan.

The Wreath winter cardigan is perfect for Christmas parties and glistening walks in the snow. The cuffs are knitted in twisted rib and decorated with Latvian braids, which makes them look extra special.

Yarn: Léttlopi from Ístex (100% Icelandic wool, 50 g = 100 m/109 yd)
Tension: 18 sts × 24 rows in stocking stitch in pattern using 5 mm (US 8) needles = 10 × 10 cm
Sizes: XS (S) M (L) XL (2XL) 3XL (4XL)
Bust: 85 (94) 98 (107) 120 (134) 143 (156) cm/ 33½ (37) 38½ (42¼) 47¼ (52¾) 56¼ (61½) in
Length: 55 (55.5) 59 (60) 63 (64.5) 66.5 (68) cm/21¾ (21¾) 23¼ (23½) 24¾ (25½) 26¼ (26¾) in
Sleeve length: 44 (45) 47 (49) 51 (52) 52 (52) cm/17¼ (17¾) 18½ (19¼) 20 (20½) 20½ (20½) in
Amounts: Colour 1 = 350 (400) 450 (500) (500) 550 (600) (600) g Light Ash Heather (no. 10054)
Colour 2 = 150 (150) 150 (150) 150 (150) 200 (200) g Pine Green Heather (no. 11407)
Double-pointed needles: 4.5 mm (US 7) and 5 mm (US 8)
Circular needles: 4.5 mm (US 7) and 5 mm (US 8), 80 cm
Notions: 10 buttons (15 mm in diameter), stitch holder, decorative band (optional)
Difficulty level: 3 of 3
Construction: Body and sleeves are knitted bottom up in the round separately and are then placed on the same circular needle. Then the yoke is knitted with a colourwork band, decreases, back short rows and a neckband. To finish, the cardigan is cut open (see Knitting School, page 160) after the button bands are knitted on. Note that the hem and neckband are knitted back and forth.
Techniques: Since the steek stitches are cast on in conjunction with row 1 in the Latvian braid it's recommended they are cast on with every other stitch in colour 1 and every other stitch in colour 2.
k1tbl = twisted knit stitch. Knit the stitch through the back loop.
p1tbl = twisted purl stitch. Purl the stitch through the back loop.
M1L = increase 1 st slanting left, see Knitting School, page 163.
M1R = increase 1 st slanting right, see Knitting School, page 163.

Body

With 4.5 mm circular needle and colour 2: Cast on 145 (161) 173 (189) 213 (233) 249 (273) sts.

Work twisted rib back and forth:

Row 1 (WS): *p1tbl, k1*, repeat from *–* to last 1 st, 1 p1tbl.
Row 2 (RS): *k1tbl, p1*, repeat from *–* to last 1 st, 1 k1tbl.
Row 3 (WS): *p1tbl, k1*, repeat from *–* to last 1 st, 1 p1tbl.

Repeat rows 2 and 3 until the rib measures 5 cm.

N.B. Finish the rib with a WS row.

LATVIAN BRAID

Rnd 1 (RS): With 5 mm circular needle and colour 2, k1 *k1 with colour 1, k1 with colour 2*. Repeat from *–* to end of row. Then cast on 5 steek stitches using the double twisted loop technique (see video links in the Knitting School, page 164 and Techniques). Cont to knit in rnd. The steek stitches also work as a 'marker' for the beginning and end of a round. (N.B. The steek stitches don't count towards the cardigan's total stitch count, and any increases or decreases should not be made within these stitches.)

Rnd 2: p1 with colour 2, *p1 with colour 1, p1 with colour 2*. Repeat from *–* to end of rnd. N.B. Hold both threads in front of work when knitting. When changing colours the new yarn should be passed under the yarn you have just knitted with.

Rnd 3: p1 with colour 2,* p1 with colour 1, p1 with colour 2*. Repeat from *–* to end of rnd. N.B. Hold both threads in front of work when knitting. When changing colours the new yarn should be passed over the yarn you have just knitted with.

BODY, CONTINUED

With colour 1: Knit 1 rnd.

Knit and at the same time increase 8 (8) 4 (4) 4 (8) 8 (8) sts evenly spaced across the rnd = 153 (169) 177 (193) 217 (241) 257 (281) sts.

Continue in stocking stitch (= knit all rows when knitting in the round) until the body measures 25 (26) 27 (28) 29 (30) 31 (32) cm, or length of your choice. Set the work aside.

Sleeves

With 4.5 mm dpns and colour 2: Cast on40 (40) 40 (40) 40 (44) 44 (44) sts.

Work twisted rib in the round (1 k1tbl, p1) for 5 cm.

LATVIAN BRAID

Rnd 1: With 5 mm dpns *k1 with colour 2, k1 with colour 1*. Repeat from *–* to end of rnd.

Rnd 2: *p1 with colour 2, p1 with colour 1*. Repeat from *–* to end of row. N.B. Hold both threads in front of work when knitting. When changing colours the new yarn should be passed under the yarn you have just knitted with.

Rnd 3: *p1 with colour 2, p1 with colour 1*. Repeat from *–* to end of rnd. N.B. Hold both threads in front of work when knitting. When changing colours the new yarn should be passed over the yarn you have just knitted with.

With colour 1: Knit 1 rnd. Place marker at beg of rnd.

Continue in stocking stitch and at the same time increase 8 (8) 8 (8) 8 (4) 4 (4) sts evenly spaced across the rnd = 48 (48) 48 (48) 48 (48) 48 (48) sts.

With colour 1: Knit 14 rnds.

Inc rnd: * k1, M1L (see Techniques), knit to last 1 stitch on the rnd, M1R (see Techniques), k1.

Knit 19 (13) 9 (7) 5 (3) 3 (3) rnds without increases.*

Repeat from *–* 2 (4) 6 (10) 14 (18) 21 (23) times in total = 52 (56) 60 (68) 76 (84) 90 (94) sts.

Knit until the sleeve measures 44 (45) 47 (49) 51 (52) 52 (52) cm, or length of your choice.

Next rnd: Knit to last 4 (5) 5 (6) 7 (7) 8 (8) sts on the row. Place the following 8 (10) 10 (12) 14 (14) 16 (16) sts on a stitch holder/scrap yarn (= underarm armhole stitches).

Cut the yarn and place the sleeve's remaining 44 (46) 50 (56) 62 (70) 74 (78) sts on a stitch holder.

Set the work aside and make a second sleeve the same way.

Join body and sleeves

Continue knitting in the round in stocking stitch.

With 5 mm circular needle and colour 1: Knit right front 34 (37) 39 (42) 47 (53) 56 (62) sts. Place the following 8 (10) 10 (12) 14 (14) 16 (16) sts on a stitch holder. Knit right sleeve 44 (46) 50 (56) 62 (70) 74 (78) sts. Knit the back 69 (75) 79 (85) 95 (107) 113 (125) sts. Place the following 8 (10) 10 (12) 14 (14) 16 (16) sts on a stitch holder. Knit left sleeve 44 (46) 50 (56) 62 (70) 74 (78) sts. Knit left front 34 (37) 39 (42) 47 (53) 56 (62) sts = 225 (241) 257 (281) 313 (353) 373 (405) sts on the needle.

Knit 1 rnd.

Next rnd, sizes **XS, S, M, 2XL:** Knit. Sizes **L, XL, 3XL, 4XL:** Decrease 8 (8) 4 (4) sts evenly spaced = 225 (241) 257 (273) 305 (353) 369 (401) sts.

Yoke

Knit 11 (12) 13 (14) 16 (17) 18 (19) rnds.

Dec rnd 1: k1, *k6, k2tog*. Repeat from *–* to end of rnd = 197 (211) 225 (239) 267 (309) 323 (351) sts. Knit 5 rows.

Decrease rnd 2, sizes **XS, M** and **2XL:** k7, *k2tog, k12*. Repeat from *–* to last 8 sts on the rnd, k2tog, k6 = 183 (-) 209 (-) - (287) - (-) sts.

Dec rnd 2, sizes **S, L, XL, 3XL** and **4XL:** k7, *k2tog, k12*. Repeat from *–* to last 8 sts on the rnd, k8 = - (197) - (223) 249 (-) 301 (327) sts.

Knit 1 rnd.

Work the colour pattern according to the chart, rnds 1–12, reading chart from right to left from every rnd. For each rnd repeat stitches 2–7 (1–6) 1–6 (6–11) 5–10 (4–9) 3–8 (2–7) a total of 14 (15) 16 (18) 20 (23) 24 (26) times. Then knit stitches 8–22 (7–23) 7–23 (12–18) 11–19 (10–20) 9–21 (8–22) a total of 1 time. Finally repeat stitches 23–28 (24–29) 24–29 (19–24) 21–26 (22–27) 22–27 (23–28) for the remainder of the rnd.

Knit 1 rnd and at the same time decrease 0 (1) 0 (1) 1 (0) 1 (1) sts = 183 (196) 209 (222) 248 (287) 300 (326) sts.

Dec rnd 3: k2, *k2tog, k11*. Repeat from *–* to last 12 sts on the rnd, k2tog, k10.

Knit 2 rnds.

Dec rnd 4: k3, *k2tog, k4*. Repeat from *–* to last 4 sts on the rnd, k2tog, k2.

Knit 5 rnds.

Dec rnd 5: k3, *k2tog, 3 rm*. Repeat from *–* to last 3 sts on the rnd, k2tog, k1.

Knit 2 rnds.

Dec rnd 6: k2, *k2tog, k2*. Repeat from *–* to last 3 sts on the rnd, k2tog, k1 = 85 (91) 97 (103) 115 (133) 139 (151) sts.

Back short rows

Read about short rows and wrap and turn on page 162. Now you will knit stocking stitch back and forth with knit and purl short rows: Knit 56 (60) 64 (68) 76 (88) 92 (100), wrap and turn. Purl 28 (30) 32 (34) 38 (44) 46 (50), wrap and turn. *Knit to last 4 sts before the last turn, wrap and turn. Purl to last 4 sts before the last turn, wrap and turn*.

Repeat from *–* 2 (2) 3 (3) 4 (4) 5 (5) times in total, then knit to end of rnd at the same time picking up the wrapped stitches according to the description in the Knitting School. Work 1 row where the rest of the wrapped stitches are picked up and knitted.

Neckband

Knit 1 rnd and at the same time, decrease 4 (2) 4 (2) 2 (12) 14 (22) sts evenly spaced across the row = 81 (89) 93 (101) 113 (121) 125 (129) sts.

LATVIAN BRAID

Row 1: With circular needle 5 mm and colour 2, k1 *k1 with colour 1, k1 with colour 2*. Repeat from *–* to end of row.

Row2: p1 with colour 2,*p1 with colour 1, p1 with colour 2*. Repeat from *–* to end of row. N.B. Hold both threads in front of work when knitting. When changing colours the new yarn should be passed under the yarn you have just knitted with.

Row3: p1 with colour 2,*p1 with colour 1, p1 with colour 2*. Repeat from *–* to end of row. N.B. Hold both threads in front of work when knitting. When changing colours the new yarn should be passed over the yarn you have just knitted with.

NECKBAND, CONTINUED

Change to 4.5 mm circular needle and cast off the 5 steek stitches at the middle of the front. Then work in twisted rib back and forth:

Row 1 (RS): Knit.

Row 2 (WS): *p1tbl, k1*, repeat from *–* to last 1 st, p1tbl.

Row 3 (RS): *k1tbl, p1*, repeat from *–* to last 1 st, k1tbl.

Row 4 (WS): *p1tbl, k1*, repeat from *–* to last 1 st, p1tbl.

Repeat rows 3 and 4 until the rib measures 4 cm. Finish with a wrong-side row.

Dec row: *k1tbl, p1, k2tog tbl*. Repeat from *–* 19 (21) 22 (24) 27 (29) 30 (31) times and finish in rib to end of row.

Knit sleeve and body stitches together

With 3.5 mm dpns: Knit the stitches together from the sleeves and the body underneath the armholes using the 3-needle cast off method (see Knitting School, page 164). Weave in loose ends.

Button bands

LEFT BUTTON BAND

With 4.5 mm circular needle and colour 2 (RS): Pick up stitches along the left front edge starting from the top. To make the edge flexible, pick up 2 of 3 sts (= *knit 2 st, skip the 3rd st*, repeat from *–*). Make sure to have an odd number of stitches. Now work in twisted rib:

Row 1 (WS): *p1tbl, k1*, repeat from *–* to last 1 st, p1tbl.

Row 2 (RS): *k1tbl, p1*, repeat from *–* to last 1 st, k1tbl.

Row 3 (WS): *p1tbl, k1*, repeat from *–* to last 1 st, p1tbl.

Repeat rows 2 and 3, 4 times in total (= 9 rows in total). Cast off in rib.

RIGHT BUTTON BAND

With 4.5 mm circular needle and colour 2 (RS): Pick up stitches along the right front edge starting from the bottom. Make sure to pick up the same number of stitches as on left button band. Distribute 10 buttonholes evenly over the edge and place markers on needle. (Each buttonhole goes over 2 sts.)

Work in twisted rib according to the instructions for the left button band up to and including row 3.

Row 4 (buttonhole row 1, RS): Work in rib to the first buttonhole. Then work as follows: *Cast off 2 sts, continue in rib pattern to the next buttonhole*. Repeat from *–* until you have made a start on all buttonholes, then work in rib to end of row.

Row 5 (buttonhole row 2, WS): Work in rib as set to the first buttonhole and finish as follows:

Cast on 2 sts using the double twisted loop technique, continue in established rib to next buttonhole. Repeat from *–* until all buttonholes have been finished and then work in rib to end of row.

Work 4 rows twisted rib and then cast off in rib.

Cutting the steek

See page 160. Sew a reinforcing seam with sewing thread (by hand using backstitch), on each side of the middle steek stitch. Carefully cut the cardigan open in the middle of the middle steek stitch. (The cut edges will roll in towards the wrong side.)

Finishing

Weave in loose ends. Block the cardigan carefully according to the instructions in the Knitting School, page 161. Sew in buttons in height with the buttonholes. Either cover the cut edges on the inside with a decorative band, or fold them in and sew with discreet stitches to the wrong side (see pages 160–161).

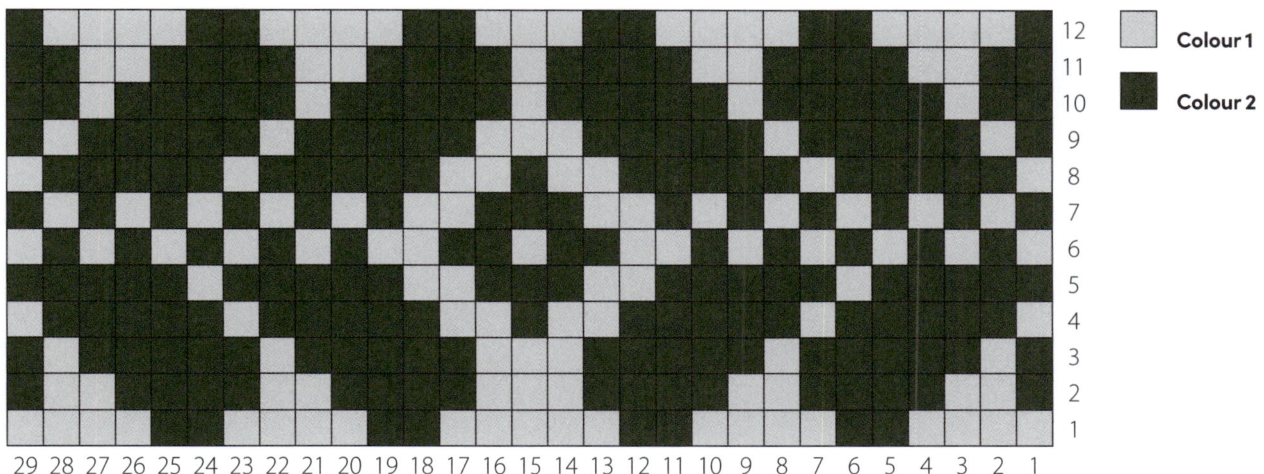

Christmas in Bergslagen

I have spent many Christmases in Guldsmedshyttan – the village of my childhood. When the Råsvalen lake has frozen, a peaceful calm takes hold of the old mining community. The church stands majestically, and the lights shine brightly in Bergsgården's windows. At home, Dad has lit a fire and the cast iron stove crackles cosily while the old floor clock ticks calmly. Mum has brought out the exquisite porcelain Christmas angel, the one that grandma was gifted when she was little. This is how a Christmas in Bergslagen should be celebrated. Low-key and comfortable, without too much effort.

Christmas in Bergslagen is a short dress cardigan to be worn over the holiday. You can make it extra dazzling with big, festive buttons. I had saved these red vintage ones for mine.

Yarn: Svensk Ull 3-ply from Järbo (100% Swedish wool, 100 g = 180 m/196 yd)
Tension: 21 sts × 28 rows in stocking stitch in pattern using 4 mm (US 6) needles = 10 × 10 cm
Sizes: XS (S) M (L) XL (2XL) 3XL (4XL)
Bust: 80 (88) 96 (104) 116 (128) 140 (152) cm/ 31½ (34¾) 37¾ (41) 45¾ (50½) 55 (59¾) in
Length: 38 (40) 42 (45) 48 (53) 57 (60) cm/15 (15¾) 16½ (17¾) 19 (20¾) 22½ (23½) in
Sleeve length: 15 (15) 15 (16) 16 (17) 17 (17) cm/ 6 (6) 6 (6¼) 6¼ (6¾) 6¾ (6¾) in
Amounts: Colour 1 = 250 (250) 300 (350) 350 (350) 450 (550) g Wasa Crisp (no. 59021)
Colour 2 = 100 (100) 100 (100) 100 (100) 100 (100) g Lingonberry Jam (no. 59018)
Double-pointed needles: 3.5 mm (US 4) and 4 mm (US 6)
Circular needles: 3.5 mm (US 4) and 4 mm (US 6), 60 cm
Notions: 5 buttons (25 mm), 4 stitch markers, stitch holder
Difficulty level: 3 of 3
Construction: The cardigan is waist-length with a colourwork band at the bottom of the body. It has short sleeves and is knitted from the bottom up in one piece. To finish, the cardigan is cut open (see Knitting School, page 160) after button bands are knitted on.
Techniques: M1L = increase 1 st slanting left, see Knitting School, page 163.
M1R = increase 1 st slanting right, see Knitting School, page 163.
p2tog tbl = knit 2 twisted purl stitches together. Slip two stitches knitwise, transfer the stitches back onto the left needle and purl together through the back loop.
SM = slip marker, see Knitting School, page 163.
Raglan decreases on purl rows = Work to last 3 sts before marker, p2tog tbl, p1, SM, p1, p2tog*. Repeat from *–*another 3 times = 8 sts decreased.

Body

With 3.5 mm circular needle and colour 1: Cast on 169 (181) 193 (217) 229 (265) 289 (313) sts.

Work in rib back and forth:

Row 1 (WS): *p1, k1*, repeat from *–* to last 1 st, p1.
Row 2 (RS): *k1, p1*, repeat from *–* to last 1 st, k1.
Row 3 (WS): *p1, k1*, repeat from *–* to last 1 st, p1.

Repeat rows 2 and 3 until the rib measures 4 cm. N.B. Finish the rib with a wrong side row.

From now, the body is knitted in the round in stocking stitch (= knit all rows when knitting in the round).

With 4 mm circular needle: Knit to end of row. Cast on 5 steek stitches using the double twisted loop technique (see video links in Knitting School, page 164). The steek stitches also work as a marker for the beginning and end of a rnd. (Note that the steek stitches don't count towards the cardigan's total stitch count, and any increases or decreases should not be made within these stitches.)

Knit 1 rnd.

Knit the colour pattern according to the chart, reading the chart from right to left, rnds 1–27 with the following placement for each size, **XS:** knit stitches 1–24 a total of 7 times, then stitch 1 (**S:** knit stitches 19–24, then 1–24 a total of 7 times, then stitches 1–7) **M:** knit stitches 1–24 a total of 8 times, then stitch 1 (**L:** knit stitches 1–24 a total of 9 times, then stitch 1) **XL:** knit stitches 19–24, then 1–24 a total of 9 times, then stitches 1–7 (**2XL:** knit stitches 1–24 a total of 11 times, then stitch 1) **3XL:** knit stitches 1–24 a total of 12 times, then stitch 1 (**4XL:** knit stitches 1–24 total 13 times, then stitch 1).

With colour 1: Knit 2 rnds.

Following rnd, **XS, M, XL:** Increase 4 (-) 4 (-) 2 (-) - (-) sts evenly spaced. **L, 2XL, 3XL** and **4XL:** Decrease 4 sts evenly spaced = 173 (181) 197 (213) 231 (261) 285 (309) sts. N.B. No increasing/ decreasing in done for size **S**.

Continue knitting until the body measures 24 (25) 25 (26) 26 (28) 29 (31) cm, or length of your choice. Set the work aside.

Sleeves

With 3.5 mm dpns and colour 1: Cast on 48 (50) 56 (62) 72 (82) 92 (102) sts.

Work in the round in rib stitch (k1, p1) for 4 cm. Place marker at beg of rnd.

Change to 4 mm dpns and continue knitting in stocking stitch in the rnd (= knit all rows when knitting in the round), at the same time increase 10 (10) 10 (10) 10 (10) 10 (10) sts evenly spaced across the rnd = 58 (60) 66 (72) 82 (92) 102 (112) sts.

Knit 2 rnds.

Increase rnd: *k1, M1L (see Techniques), knit to last 1 stitch on the rnd, M1R (see Techniques), k1.

Knit 2 rnds *.

Repeat from *–* 5 times = 68 (70) 76 (82) 92 (102) 112 (122) sts. Knit until the sleeve measures 15 (15) 15 (16) 16 (17) 17 (17) cm, or length of your choice.

Next rnd: knit until last 3 (4) 4 (5) 5 (6) 7 (8) sts on the rnd, place the following 6 (8) 8 (10) 10 (12) 12 (14) sts onto a stitch holder/ length of yarn (= armhole stitches).

Cut the yarn, place the sleeve's remaining 62 (62) 68 (72) 82 (90) 100 (108) sts on a stitch holder. Set the work aside and make second sleeve the same way.

Join body and sleeves

Continue knitting in the round in stocking stitch.

With 5 mm circular needle and colour 1: Knit right front 40 (41) 45 (48) 52 (59) 64 (69) sts. Place marker (see Knitting School, page 163) and put the following 6 (8) 8 (10) 10 (12) 14 (16) sts on a stitch holder. Knit right sleeve 62 (62) 68 (72) 82 (90) 100 (108) sts and place marker. Knit the back 81 (83) 91 (97) 107 (119) 129 (139) sts. Place marker and place the following 6 (8) 8 (10) 10 (12) 14 (16) sts on a stitch holder. Knit left sleeve 62 (62) 68 (72) 82 (90) 100 (108) sts and place marker. Knit left front 40 (41) 45 (49) 53 (60) 65 (70) sts = 285 (289) 317 (337) 375 (417) 457 (493) sts on the needle.

Knit 2 (3) 3 (4) 4 (4) 5 (5) rnds.

Raglan decreases

Dec rnd, raglan: *Knit to last 3 sts before marker, k2tog, k1, SM (see Techniques), k1, slip 1 st knitwise, k1 and pass the slipped stitch over the knitted stitch.*. Repeat from *–* another 3 times = 8 sts decreased.

Decrease the same way every other row at total of 10 (10) 12 (13) 15 (16) 18 (18) times, then every row another 8 (8) 9 (10) 10 (13) 14 (15) times = 141 (145) 149 (153) 175 (185) 201 (229) sts. N.B. Make the last decrease rnd as follows: Knit to last 8 (9) 10 (11) 12 (13) 14 (15) sts before the steek stitches. Then cast off for neckline, see next section.

Neckline

Cast off 21 (23) 25 (27) 29 (31) 33 (35) sts (N.B. The number of stitches includes the 5 steek stitches that are cast off in conjunction with shaping the neckband) = 125 (127) 129 (131) 151 (159) 163 (199) sts.

Now the remainder of the yoke is worked in stocking stitch back and forth.

Continue making raglan decrease every row. (For raglan decreases on wrong side rows, see Techniques on page 128.)

AT THE SAME TIME, shape the neckline gradually as follows:

Row 1 and 2: Cast off 4 sts at the beginning of both rows = 101 (103) 105 (107) 127 (135) 139 (175) sts.
Row 3 and 4: Cast off 3 sts at the beginning of both rows = 79 (81) 83 (85) 105 (113) 117 (153) sts.
Row 5 and 6: Cast off 2 (2) 2 (2) 2 (3) 3 (3) sts at the beginning of both rows = 59 (61) 63 (65) 85 (91) 95 (131) sts.
Row 7 and 8: Cast off 1 (1) 1 (1) 2 (2) 2 (2) sts at the beginning of both rows = 41 (43) 45 (47) 65 (71) 75 (111) sts.
Row 9 and 10: Cast off 1 (1) 1 (1) 2 (2) 2 (2) sts at the beginning of both rows = 23 (25) 27 (29) 43 (51) 55 (79) sts.

Now the raglan decreases and neckline are completed for sizes **XS–L**.

XL, 2XL, 3XL and **4XL:** On rows 11 and 12, cast off 1 st at the beginning of both rows. N.B. No raglan decreases are done on row 12 for size **XL** = - (-) - (-) 33 (33) 37 (73) sts.

Now the raglan decreases and neckline are done for sizes **XL–3XL**.

4XL: On rows 13 and 14 cast off 1 st at the beginning of both rows = - (-) - (-) - (-) - (55) sts. A total of 23 (25) 27 (29) 33 (33) 37 (55) sts remain on the needle.

Neckband

From the right side with 3.5 mm circular needle and colour 1: Pick up 16 (17) 18 (19) 21 (21) 26 (30) new stitches along right front neckline. Knit the remaining neck stitches and then pick up 16 (17) 18 (19) 21 (21) 26 (30) new stitches from the left front neckline, so that the total number of stitches is 55 (59) 63 (67) 75 (75) 89 (115).

Work back and forth:

Row 1 (WS): *p1, k1*. Repeat from *–* to last 1 st, p1.
Row 2 (RS): *k1, p1*. Repeat from *–* to last 1 st, k1.
Row 3 (WS): *p1, k1*. Repeat *–* to last 1 st, p1.

Repeat rows 2 and 3, four times in total. Finish with a wrong-side row.

Cast off loosely in rib.

Button bands

LEFT BUTTON BAND

With 3.5 mm circular needle and colour 1 (RS): Pick up stitches along the left front edge starting from the top. To make the edge flexible, pick up 2 of 3 sts (= *knit 2 sts, skip the 3rd st*, repeat from *–*). Make sure you have an odd number of stitches.

Now work in rib stitch:

Row 1 (WS): *p1, k1*, repeat from *–* to last 1 st, p1.
Row 2 (RS): *k1, p1*, repeat from *–* to last 1 st, k1.
Row 3 (WS): *p1, k1*, repeat from *–* to last 1 st, p1.

Repeat rows 2 and 3 a total of 5 times = a total of 11 rows.
Cast off in rib.

RIGHT BUTTON BAND

With 3.5 mm circular needle and colour 1 (RS): Pick up stitches along the right front edge starting from the bottom. Make sure to pick up the same number of stitches as on the left side. Distribute 5 buttonholes evenly across the edge and place markers on the needle. (Each buttonhole goes over 3 sts.)

Work in rib according to the instructions for the left side up to and including row 5.

Row 6 (buttonhole row 1, RS): Work in rib to the first buttonhole. Then work as follows: *Cast off 3 sts, continue in rib as set to the next buttonhole*. Repeat from *–* until you have completed all buttonholes, then work in rib to end of row.

Row 7 (buttonhole row 2, WS): Work in rib to the first buttonhole and finish as follows: *Cast on 3 sts using the double twisted loop technique and continue in rib as set to next buttonhole. *Repeat from *–* until all buttonholes have been finished and then work in rib to end of row.

Work another 4 rows in rib and then cast off in rib.

Cutting the steek

See Knitting School, page 160. Sew a reinforcing seam with sewing thread (by hand using backstitch), on each side of the middle steek stitch. Carefully cut the cardigan open in the middle of the middle steek stitch. (The cut edges will roll in towards the wrong side.)

Colour 1

Colour 2

Finishing

Sew any gaps in the underarm together using kitchener stitch. Weave in loose ends. Block the cardigan carefully according to the instructions in the Knitting School. Either cover the cut edges on the inside using a decorative band, or fold them in and sew with discreet stitches to the wrong side (see Knitting School, pages 160–161).

Jewellery

WINTER

The Jewellery cardigan came about when I thought about a knitted garment also being a kind of jewellery. I was brought up in a home where jewellery craft was always present in everyday life, since both of my parents are goldsmiths. Jewellery is wearable art. You can wear jewellery pieces close to your heart. Perhaps they make you reminiscence about times gone by or maybe you feel extra dressed up when you wear them.

For me, it's the same with cardigans and they hold the same kind of magic. This cardigan is adorned with a lace-knitted yoke which, like a pearl necklace, rests around your neck.

The yarn for this cardigan is unspun and working with such a yarn requires careful handling. Make sure not to pull the wheel hard when feeding the thread. If the yarn breaks you can easily mend it by splicing: dampen your hands, place the ends over each other and twist them together again.

Yarn: Plötulopi from Ístex (100% Icelandic wool, 100 g = 300 m/327 yd)
Tension: 19 sts × 26 rows in stocking stitch using 4 mm (US 6) needles = 10 × 10 cm
Sizes: S (M) L (XL) 2XL
Bust: 100 (108) 116 (124) 132 cm/39¼ (42½) 45¾ (48¾) 52
Length: 50 (52) 54 (57) 60 cm/19¾ (20½) 21¼ (22½) 23½ in
Sleeve length: 39 (40) 41 (41) 42 cm/15¼ (15¾) 16¼ (16¼) 16½ in
Amounts: 300 (300) 350 (400) 500 g Ivory Beige (no. 1038)
Double-pointed needles: 3.5 mm (US 4) and 4 mm (US 6)
Circular needles: 3.5 mm (US 4) and 4 mm (US 6), 80 cm
Notions: stitch holder, 11 buttons (15 mm in diameter), decorative band (optional)
Difficulty level: 3 of 3
Construction: The cardigan is knitted in the round from the top down with a lace pattern on the yoke. When the yoke is finished, short rows are knitted on the back panel to raise the neck at the back. Then body and sleeves are knitted. Finally, the cardigan is cut open (see Knitting School, page 160) after the button bands are knitted on. Note that the hem and neckband are knitted back and forth.

Yoke

NECKBAND

With circular needle 3.5 mm: Cast on 107 (109) 111 (111) 113 sts.

Row 1 (WS): p1, *k1, p1*, repeat from *–* to end of row.

Row 2 (RS): k1, *p1, k1*, repeat from *–* to end of row.

Row 3 (WS): p1, *k1, p1*, repeat from *–* to end of row.

Repeat rows 2 and 3 until the rib measures 4 cm.

From now the work is knitted in the round.

Change to 4 mm circular needle: Knit at the same time increase 1 (8) 15 (15) 22 sts evenly spaced across the row = 108 (117) 126 (126) 135 sts.

Cast on 5 steek stitches using the double twisted loop technique (see video links in Knitting School, page 164). The steek stitches also work as a marker for the beginning and end of a rnd. (Note that the steek stitches don't count towards the cardigan's total stitch count, and any increases or decreases should not be made within these stitches.)

Knit rnds 2–30 in the chart and increase as indicated on the chart (start at stitch 8 of chart and follow chart from right to left for each rnd) = 276 (299) 322 (322) 344 sts.

Knit in stocking stitch (= knit all rows when knitting in the round) until the work measures 25 (26) 27 (27) 28 cm from the neckline.

Divide for the sleeves

Knit 40 (43) 48 (48) 51 st (= left front), place left sleeve 58 (64) 66 (66) 70 sts on a stitch holder/scrap yarn. Using the double twisted loop technique, cast on 8 (8) 8 (12) 12 sts for left armhole, place marker A (see Knitting School, page 163). Using the double twisted loop technique, cast on another 8 (8) 8 (12) 12 sts. Knit 80 (85) 94 (94) 102 sts (= back), place right sleeve 58 (64) 66 (66) 70 sts on a stitch holder. Using the double twisted loop technique, cast on 8 (8) 8 (12) 12 sts for right armhole, place marker B. Using the double twisted loop technique, cast on another 8 (8) 8 (12) 12 sts, knit the remaining 40 (43) 48 (48) 51 st (= right front). Now you should have 192 (203) 222 (238) 252 sts on the needle in total.

Body

Start the body with short rows. Read about short rows and wrap and turn on page 162.

Short row 1 (RS): Knit to stitch marker B, wrap and turn.

Short row 2 (WS): Purl to stitch marker A, wrap and turn.

Short row 3 (RS): Knit to the wrapped stitch, knit the wrapped stitch together with the next stitch, wrap and turn.

Short row 4: Purl to the wrapped stitch, purl the wrapped stitch together with the next stitch, wrap and turn.

Repeat rows 3–4 another 4 times (= 12 short rows have been worked in total). Then knit the remaining part of the rnd.

Continue working in stocking stitch (= knit all rows when knitting in the round) until the body measures 23 (24) 25 (28) 30 cm from the armhole.

Knit 1 more rnd and decrease 1 (0) 1 (1) 1 = 191 (203) 221 (237) 251 sts.

Knit another 1 rnd and cast off 5 steek stitches at the end.

Change to circular needle 3.5 mm and work the hem back and forth in rib stitch.

Row 1 (RS): k1, *p1, k1*, repeat from *–* to end of row.

Row 2 (WS): p1, *k1, p1* repeat from *–* to end of row.

Repeat rows 1 and 2 until the rib measures 4 cm.

Cast off loosely in rib.

Sleeves

Distribute the 58 (64) 66 (66) 70 sleeve stitches over 4 mm dpns. Pick up 10 (9) 10 (11) 11 new stitches, starting in the centre underarm of the sleeve, then knit 58 (64) 66 (66) 70 sts and then pick up 10 (9) 10 (11) 11 sts more underarm of the sleeve, ending in the centre = 78 (82) 86 (86) 92 sts. Place a stitch marker at the beginning of the row and knit in the round in stocking stitch. (= knit all rows when knitting in the round).

Knit until the sleeve measures 36 (37) 38 (38) 39 cm from the armhole.

Dec rnd: *k2tog*, repeat from *–* to last 2 (2) 2 (2) 0 sts on the rnd, knit 2 (2) 2 (2) 0 sts = 40 (42) 44 (44) 46 sts.

Change to 3.5 mm circular needles and knit in the round in rib (k1, p1) for 4 cm. Cast off loosely in rib. Make one more sleeve the same way.

Button bands

LEFT BUTTON BAND

With 4 mm circular needle (RS): Pick up stitches along the left front edge starting from the top. To make sure the edge is flexible, pick up 3 of 4 sts (= * knit 3 sts, skip the 4th stitch*, repeat from *–*). Make sure you have an odd number of stitches.

Now work in rib stitch:

Row 1 (WS): *p1, k1*, repeat from *–* to last 1 st, p1.

Row 2 (RS): *k1, p1*, repeat from *–* to last 1 st, k1.

Row 3 (WS): *p1, k1*, repeat from *–* to last 1 st, p1.

Repeat rows 2 and 3 total 3 times. Cast off in rib.

RIGHT BUTTON BAND

With 4 mm circular needle (RS): Pick up stitches along the right front edge starting from the bottom. Make sure to pick up the same number of stitches as on the left side. Distribute 11 buttonholes evenly across the edge, placing markers on the needle. (Each buttonhole goes over 2 sts.)

Work in rib according to the description for the left button band to row 3.

Row 4 (buttonhole row 1, RS): Work in rib to the first buttonhole. Then work as follows:

yo, k2tog, continue in established rib pattern to the next buttonhole. Repeat from *–* until all buttonholes have been finished and then work in rib stitch to end of row.

Row 5 (buttonhole row 2, WS): Work in established rib to end of row. Work another 2 rows in rib and then cast off in rib.

Cutting the steek

See Knitting School, page 160. Sew a reinforcing seam with sewing thread (by hand using backstitch), on each side of the middle steek stitch. Carefully cut the cardigan open in the middle of the middle steek stitch. (The cut edges will roll in towards the wrong side.)

Finishing

Weave in loose ends. Block the cardigan carefully according to the instructions in the Knitting School, page 161. Sew on buttons to correspond with the buttonholes. Either cover the cut edges on the inside with a decorative band, or fold them in and sew with discreet stitches to the wrong side (see Knitting School, pages 160-161).

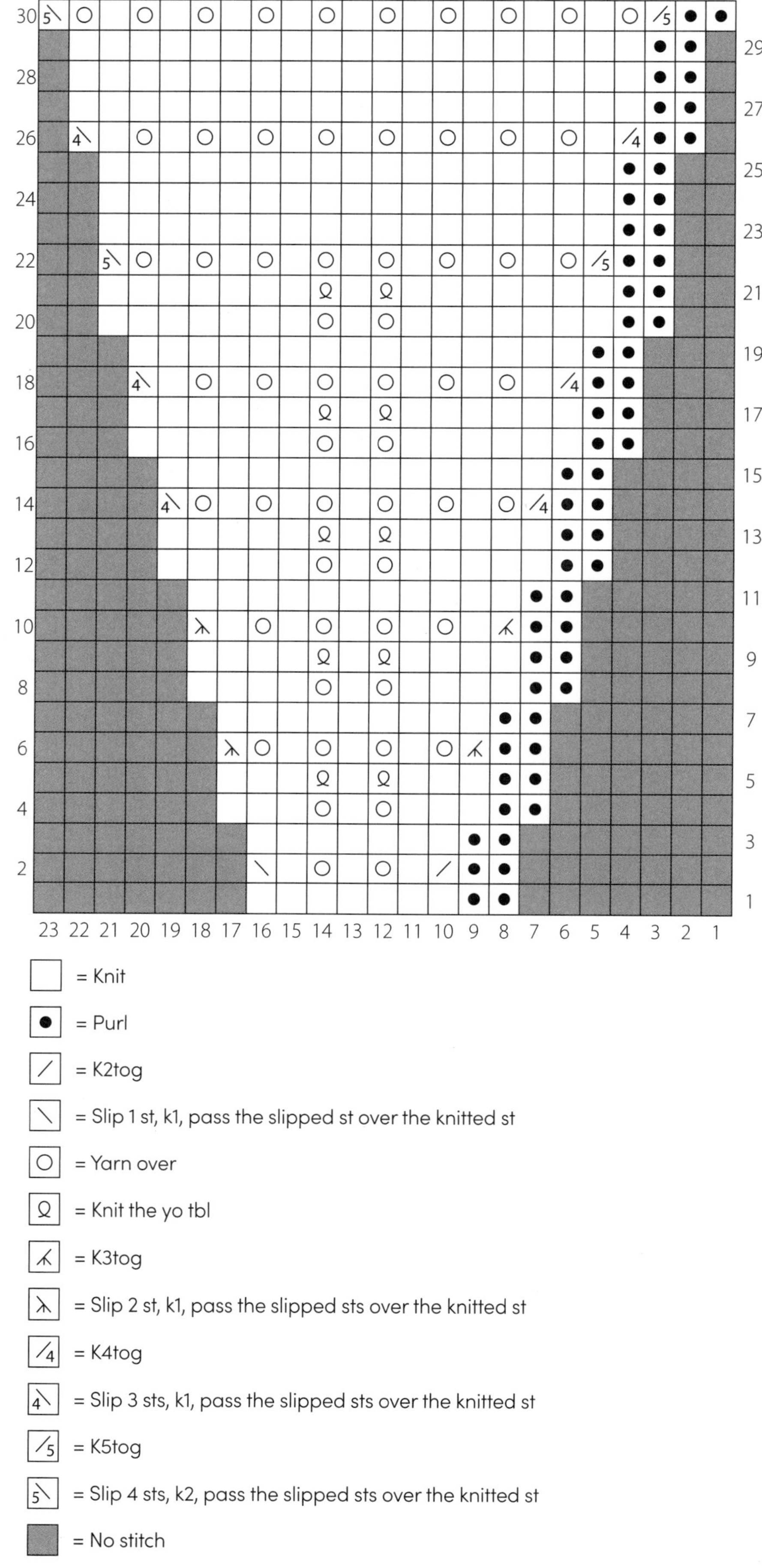
= Knit
= Purl
= K2tog
= Slip 1 st, k1, pass the slipped st over the knitted st
= Yarn over
= Knit the yo tbl
= K3tog
= Slip 2 st, k1, pass the slipped sts over the knitted st
= K4tog
= Slip 3 sts, k1, pass the slipped sts over the knitted st
= K5tog
= Slip 4 sts, k2, pass the slipped sts over the knitted st
= No stitch

Skathi

WINTER

Skathi, or Skade, is the goddess of hunting and skiing according to Old Norse mythology. She is at home in the mountains where she hunts with bow and arrow. The legend says that for a short time she was married to the sea god Njord. However, the marriage wasn't very happy. Njord longed for the sea and the seagulls and Skathi for the mountains and the wolves, so she returned home and lived alone on her father's estate instead. I love to conjure the image of how she skis there among the mountains!

The Skathi cardigan is inspired by the white mountain landscape, fit for Skathi herself. It is shaped with help from a cable section at the bottom of the body and it has cable cuffs at the sleeves. If you haven't knitted cables before Skathi is a good place to start!

Yarn: Järbo 2-ply ull (100% wool, 100 g = 300 m/327 yd)
Tension: 21 sts × 28 rows in stocking stitch using 4 mm (US 6) needles = 10 × 10 cm
Sizes: S (M) L (XL)
Bust: 90 (100) 110 (120) cm/35½ (39¼) 43¼ (47¼) in
Length: 45 (45) 46 (46) cm/17¾ (17¾) 18 (18) in
Sleeve length: 45 (46) 47 (48) cm/17¾ (18) 18½) 19 in
Amounts: 300 (350) 400 (450) g Nostalgia (no. 74103)
Circular needles: 3.5 mm (US 4) and 4 mm (US 6), 60cm
Double-pointed needles: 3.5 mm (US 4) and 4 mm (US 6)
Notions: 16 buttons (15 mm in diameter), 12 stitch markers, cable needle, stitch holder
Difficulty level: 3 of 3
Construction: The cardigan is seamless and is knitted from the top down, back and forth, in one piece. The puff sleeves are shaped with increases and decreases gradually along the work. The buttons are placed at the back.
Techniques: SM = slip marker, see Knitting School 163.

INCREASES, RIGHT SIDE

M1R = increase 1 st slanting right, see Knitting School, page 163.
M1b = increase 1 st in the stich below, see Knitting School, page 163.

CORRESPONDING INCREASES, WRONG SIDE

M1PR = pick up the thread between 2 sts from the back with the left needle and purl through the front loop.
M1PL = pick up the thread between 2 sts from the front with the left needle and purl through the back loop.

CABLES

Cable 6 sts left = slip 3 sts onto the cable needle and hold at front of work, k3, knit the 3 sts from the cable needle.
Cable 13 sts left = slip 6 sts onto the cable needle and hold at front of work, p1, k6 and then knit the 6 sts from the cable needle.

CABLE PATTERN 1 (the pattern is repeated over 7 + 1 sts).

Rows 1 and 3 (RS): *p1, k6*, repeat from *–* to last 1 st, p1.
Row 2 and other wrong side rows: Knit on knit stitches and purl on purl stitches.
Row 5: *p1, cable 6 sts left*. Repeat from *–* to last 1 st on the row, p1.
Row 6: As row 2. The pattern is repeated rows 1–6.

CABLE PATTERN 2 (the pattern is repeated over 28 + 15 m).

Rows 1, 3, 5, 7, 9 (RS): *p1, k6, p1, k6*. Repeat from *–* to last 1 st on the row, p1.
Row 2 and other wrong side rows: Knit on knit stitches and purl on purl stitches.
Row 11: *p1, cable 13 sts left, p1, k6, p1, k6*. Repeat from *–* to last 15 sts on the row, p1, cable 13 sts left, p1.
Row 12: As row 2. The pattern is repeated rows 1–12.

Yoke

CABLE EDGE

N.B. First the cable edge is knitted separately as a vertical piece, then the stitches for the yoke are picked up along its side edge.
With 4 mm needle: Cast on 6 sts.

Row 1 (WS): k2, k4.
Row 2 (RS): k4, p2.
Row 3 (WS): k2, k4.
Row 4: Place 2 sts on a cable needle and hold the needle at back of work, k2, then knit the 2 sts on the cable needle, p2.
Row 5: k2, k4.

Repeat rows 2–5, 31 times in total.

With 4 mm circular needle: Pick up new stitches for the yoke along the cable edge. With right side facing you and the cables facing downwards, pick up 1 st in 3 out of 4 rows (approx.) – i.e. skip every 4th row (approx.) = 93 sts.

YOKE, CONTINUED

Row 1 (WS): Purl and at the same time, place stitch markers (see Knitting School, page 163) as follows: between stitches 16–17 = marker D, 28–29 = marker C, 65–66 = marker B and 77–78 = marker A.

Continue in stocking stitch when nothing else is specified. Read about short rows and wrap and turn on page 162.

Row 2 (RS, Short row): Knit to marker A, SM (see Techniques), k6, wrap and turn.
Row 3 (WS, Short row): Purl to end of row, turn.
Row 4 (Short row): Knit to marker B, SM, wrap and turn.
Row 5 (Short row): Purl to end of row.
Row 6: Knot to end of row.
Row 7 (Short row): Purl to marker D, SM, p6, wrap and turn.
Row 8 (Short row): Knit to end of row.
Row 9 (Short row): Purl to marker C, SM, wrap and turn.
Row 10 (Short row): Knit to end of row.
Row 11: Purl.
Row 12: Knit.
Row 13: Purl.

Make raglan increases as well as increases for puff sleeves:

Row 14: Knit to last 1 st before marker A, M1R (see Knitting School, page 163), k1, SM, k1, M1L (see Knitting School, page 163), (M1b) 10 times (see Knitting School, page 163), M1R, k1, slip stitch marker B, k1, M1L. Knit to last 1 st before marker C, M1R, k1, SM, k1, M1L, (M1b) 10 times, M1R, k1, slip stitch marker D, k1, M1L. Knit to end of row = 28 new stitches = 121 sts.
Row 15 (S): Purl. **(M/L/XL):** Purl to last 1 st before marker D, M1PR, p1, SM, p1, M1L. Purl to last 1 st before marker C, M1PR, p1, SM, p1, M1L. Purl to last 1 st before marker B, M1PR, p1, SM, p1, M1L. Purl to last 1 st before marker A, M1PR, p1, SM, p1, M1L. Purl to end of row.
Row 16: Knit to last 1 st before marker A, M1R, k1, SM, k1, M1L, kO (1) 1 (1), (M1b) 22 times, kO (1) 1 (1), M1R, k1, SM, k1, M1L. Knit to last 1 st before marker C, M1R, k1, SM, k1, M1L, kO (1) 1 (1), (M1b) 22 times, kO (1) 1 (1), M1R, k1, SM, k1, M1L. Knit to end of row = 173 (181) 181 (181) sts.
Row 17: As row 15.
Row 18: Knit to last 1 st before marker A, M1R, k1, SM, k1, M1L. Knit to last 1 st before marker B, M1R, k1, SM, k1, M1L. Knit to last 1 st before marker C, M1R, k1, SM, k1, M1L. Knit to last 1 st before marker D, M1R, k1, SM, k1, M1L. Knit to end of row.
Row 19 (S/M): Purl. **(L/XL):** Purl to last 1 st before marker D, M1PR, p1, SM, p1, M1PL. Purl to last 1 st before marker C, M1PR, p1, SM, p1, M1PL. Purl to last 1 st before marker B, M1PR, p1, SM, p1, M1PL. Purl to last 1 st before marker A, M1PR, p1, SM, p1, M1PL. Purl to end of row.
Row 20: As row 18.
Row 21: As row 19.
Row 22: As row 18.
Row 23: As row 19.
Row 24: As row 18.
Row 25 (S/M/L): Purl. **(XL):** Purl to last 1 st before marker D, M1PR, p1, SM, p1, M1PL. Purl to last 1 st before marker C, M1PR, p1, SM, p1, M1PL. Purl to last 1 st before marker B, M1PR, p1, SM, p1, M1PL. Purl to last 1 st before marker A, M1PR, p1, SM, p1, M1PL. Purl to end of row.
Row 26: As row 18.
Row 27 (S/M/L): Purl. **(XL):** Purl to last 1 st before marker D, M1PR, p1, SM, p1, M1PL. Purl to last 1 st before marker C, M1PR, p1, SM, p1, M1PL. Purl to last 1 st before marker B, M1PR, p1, SM, p1, M1PL. Purl to last 1 st before marker A, M1PR, p1, SM, p1, M1PL. Purl to end of row.
Row 28: As row 18.
Row 29: As row 27.
Row 30: As row 18.
Row 31: Purl.
Row 32: As row 18.
Row 33: As row 31 and at the same time place eight stitch markers for puff sleeves. **(S):** Count from marker D and place a marker between stitches 12 and 13, 23 and 24, 41 and 42, and 52 and 53. Then do the same but starting from marker B. **(M):** Count from marker D and place a stitch marker between stitches 14 and 15, 25 and 26, 43 and 44, and 54 and 55. Then do the same but starting from marker B. **(L):** Count from stitch marker D and place a marker between stitches 17 and 18, 28 and 29, 46 and 47, and 57 and 58. Then do the same but starting from marker B. **(XL):** Count from marker D and place a stitch marker between stitches 20 and 21, 31 and 32, 49 and 50, and 60 and 61. Then do the same but starting from marker B.

All sizes:

Continue raglan increases at the same time decreasing for puff sleeves:

Row 34: Knit to last 1 st before marker A, M1R, k1, SM, k1, M1L, (knit to puff sleeve marker, SM, slip 1 st, k1, pass the slipped st over the knitted st) 2 times, (knit to last 2 sts before puff sleeve marker, k2tog, SM) 2 times. Knit to last 1 st before marker B, M1R, k1, SM, k1, M1L. Knit to last 1 st before marker C, M1R, k1, SM, k1, M1L, (knit to puff sleeve marker, SM, slip 1 st, k1, pass the slipped st over the knitted st) 2 times, (Knit to last 2 sts before puff sleeve marker, k2tog, SM) 2 times. Knit to last 1 st before marker D, M1R, k1, SM, k1, M1L. Knit to end of row.
Row 35: Purl.
Row 36–45: Repeat rows 34 and 35 another 5 times = 237 (253) 277 (301) sts. Now 7 decrease rows have been made and the puff sleeve decreases are completed. Remove the puff sleeve stitch markers.
Row 46: As row 18.
Row 47: Purl.
Row 48: As row 18.
Row 49: Purl. Now the raglan increases for **XL** are completed. Total number of increases 27 = 317 sts.

Sizes **S/M/L** only:
Row 50: As row 18.
Row 51: Purl.
Row 52: As row 18.
Row 53: Purl. Now the raglan increases for **L** are completed. Total number of increases 26 = 309 sts.
Sizes **S/M** only:
Row 54: As row 18.
Row 55: Purl.
Row 56: As row 18.
Row 57: Purl. Now the raglan increases for **M** are completed. Total number of increases 25 = 301 sts.
Size **S** only:
Row 58: As row 18.
Row 59: Purl. Now the raglan increases for **S** are completed. Total number of increases 24 = 293 sts.
All sizes:
Continue increasing for the body by repeating rows 60–61 below a total of 4 (7) 10 (13) times.
Row 60: Knit to last 1 st before marker A, M1R, k1, SM. Knit to marker B, SM, k1, M1L, knit to last 1 st before marker C, M1R, k1, SM, knit to marker D, SM, k1, M1L. Knit to end of row.
Row 61: Purl.

Now you should have 309 (329) 349 (369) sts on the needle.

Divide for body and sleeves

Row 1: K45 (48) 52 (56) sts (= right front), SM (now marks the right side), place 64 (66) 68 (70) sts on a stitch holder/scrap yarn (= right sleeve), remove marker, k91 (101) 109 (117) (= back), SM (now marks the left side), place 64 (66) 68 (70) sts on a stitch holder (= left sleeve), remove marker, k45 (48) 52 (56) sts (= left front) = 181 (197) 213 (229) sts.
Row 2: Purl.

Body

Work in stocking stitch until the work measures 2 cm from the division. Finish with a wrong-side row.

Now shape the body with decreases in the sides:
Dec row (RS): *Knit to last 3 sts before the side marker, slip 1 st, k1 and pass the slipped stitch over the knitted stitch, k1, SM, k1, k2tog*. Repeat from *–* 1 time, knit to end of row = 4 sts decreased.

Continue working in stocking stitch and repeat the decrease row every 6 rows 0 (0) 1 (2) times, then every 8 rows 3 (4) 3 (2) times and then every 10 rows 1 (0) 0 (0) times = 161 (177) 193 (209) sts. Continue knitting until the work measures 14 (14) 15 (15) cm from the division. Finish with a wrong-side row.
Increase row: Increase 22 (6) 18 (2) sts evenly spaced across the row = 183 (183) 211 (211) sts.

Purl 1 row.

CABLE SECTION

Work cable pattern 1, rows 1–6, a total of 4 times (see Techniques).

Work cable pattern 2, rows 1–12, a total of 2 times (see Techniques).
Row 1 (RS): *p1, k6*, repeat from *–* to last 1 st, p1.
Row 2 (WS): *k1, p6*, repeat from *–* to last 1 st, k1.

Repeat rows 1 and 2 another 5 times = 12 rows in total.

BOTTOM RIB

Rib row: *p1, k2, p2, k2*. Repeat from *–* to last 1 st, p1.

Repeat the rib row until the work measures 4 cm. Finish with a wrong-side row.

Cast off loosely in rib pattern.

Sleeves

Divide 64 (66) 68 (70) sts over 4 mm dpns, as evenly as possible.

Join the yarn by picking up 1 st under the sleeve, k64 (66) 68 (70), pick up another 1 st under the sleeve, place a stitch marker to mark the start of the row = 66 (68) 70 (72) sts.

Knit until the sleeve measures 36 (37) 38 (39) cm. **S:** Increase 4 sts evenly spaced across the next row = 70 sts. **M:** Increase 2 sts evenly spaced across the next row = 70 sts. **L:** Knit 1 row without decreases or increases = 70 sts. **XL:** Decrease 2 sts evenly spaced across the next row = 70 sts.

CABLE CUFF

Rows 1 and 3 (RS): *p1, k6*, repeat from *–* to end of row.
Row 2 and following rows with even numbers: Knit on knit stitches and purl on purl stitches.
Row 5: *p1, cable 6 sts left *, repeat from *–* to end of row.
Row 6: As row 2.

Repeat rows 1–6, six times in total.

Cast off loosely knitwise.

Make a second sleeve the same way.

Button bands

LEFT BUTTON BAND

With 3.5 mm circular needle (RS): Pick up 130 sts evenly along the left front edge starting from the top. To make sure the edge is flexible, pick up 3 of 4 sts (= * knit 3 sts, skip the 4th stitch*, repeat from *–*).
Row 1 (WS): *p2, k2*, repeat from *–* to last 2 sts, p2.
Row 2 (RS): *k2, p2*, repeat from *–* to last 2 sts, k2.
Row 3 (WS): *Sp2, k2*, repeat from *–* to last 2 sts, p2.

Repeat rows 1 and 2 twice more = 7 rows have been worked in total. Cast off in rib.

RIGHT BUTTON BAND

With circular needle 3.5 mm (RS): Pick up 130 sts along the right front edge starting from the bottom.
Row 1 (WS): *p2, k2*, repeat from *–* to last 2 sts, p2.
Row 2 (RS): *k2, p2*, repeat from *–* to last 2 sts, k2.
Row 3 (WS): *p2, k2*, repeat from *–* to last 2 sts, p2.
Row 4 (buttonhole row 1): *k2, p2, k2, yo, k2tog*. Repeat from *–* to last 2 sts, k2. Now a total of 16 buttonholes have been made.
Row 5 (buttonhole row 2): *p2, k2*, repeat from *–* to last 2 sts, p2.

Repeat rows 1 and 2 once more = a total of 7 rows have been worked. Cast off in rib.

Finishing

Weave in loose ends. Block the cardigan carefully according to the instructions in the Knitting School, page 161. Sew on buttons to correspond with the buttonholes.

Silhouette

WINTER

Silhouette is a soft, warming extra layer to wear during the coldest months of the year. It has a neat fit so that it can be worn underneath a jumper or a jacket while it's perfect to keep on in the ski cabin in the evenings, after a long day in the tracks.

Since Silhouette is knitted in an exclusive wool and silk blend it can also be transformed into a luxurious New Year's cardigan if you, for example, choose glistening buttons and match it with pearls and a velvet skirt.

Yarn: Llama Silk from Järbo (70% soft baby lama, 30% mulberry silk, 50 g = 165 m/180 yd)
Tension: 26 sts × 37 rows in stocking stitch using 3.5 mm (US 4) needles = 10 × 10 cm
Sizes: XS (S) M (L) XL (2XL) 3XL (4XL)
Bust: 84 (92) 100 (108) 118 (128) 138 (150) cm/ 33 (36¼) 39¼ (42½) 46½ (50½) 54¼ (59) in
Length: 37 (39) 41 (43) 45 (47) 49 (51) cm/14½ (15¼) 16¼ (17) 17¾ (18½) 19¼ (20) in
Sleeve length: 45 (46) 47 (48) 49 (50) 51 (51) cm/17¾ (18) 18½ (19) 19¼ (19¾) 20 (20) in
Amounts: 250 (300) 350 (400) 450 (500) 550 (600) g Graphite Grey (no. 12206)
Circular needles: 3 mm (US 2.5) and 3.5 mm (US 4), 80 cm
Notions: 5 buttons (10–15 mm), stitch holder
Difficulty level: 2 of 3
Construction: The cardigan is knitted in five pieces that are assembled with seams in the sides.
Techniques: M1b = increase 1 st in the stich below, see Knitting School, page 163.

Back

With 3 mm circular needle: Cast on 106 (118) 126 (138) 150 (162) 174 (186) sts.

Work in rib back and forth:

Row 1 (WS): k2, *p2, k2*. Repeat from *–* to end of row.

Row 2 (RS): p2, *k2, p2*. Repeat from *–* to end of row.

Row 3: k2, *p2, k2*. Repeat from *–* to end of row. Repeat rows 2 and 3 until the work measures 5 cm ending with a WS row.

Continue in stocking stitch (= knit on right side and purl on wrong side).

Change to 3.5 mm circular needles and decrease 0 (2) 0 (2) 0 (0) 0 (0) sts on the first row = 106 (116) 126 (136) 150 (162) 174 (186) sts.

Work until the work measures 8 (9) 9 (10) 10 (10) 10 (10) cm. Finish with a wrong-side row.

Inc row: k1, M1b (see Techniques), knit to last 2 sts on the row, M1b, k1.

Repeat the increase row every 3 cm another 2 times = 112 (122) 132 (142) 156 (168) 180 (192) sts.

Continue in stocking stitch until the work measures 18 (19) 20 (21) 21 (22) 22 (23) cm. Finish with a wrong-side row.

Cast off for armholes at the sides as follows: Cast off 5 (6) 6 (7) 7 (7) 7 (7) sts at each end of next 2 rows, then cast off 3 sts at each end of the next 2 rows. Then cast off 2 sts at each end 1 (2) 3 (3) 4 (4) 4 (4) times and finally dec 1 st at each end 3 (2) 3 (4) 4 (4) 4 (4) times = 86 (92) 96 (102) 112 (124) 136 (148) sts.

Work until the armhole measures 17 (18) 19 (20) 21 (22) 23 (24) cm. Finish with a wrong-side row.

Back neck and shoulder shaping:

Form the neckline by casting off 40 (40) 40 (42) 42 (44) 46 (48) sts in the middle of the back.

Then finish each side separately as follows:

Left neck and shoulder:

Cast off 2 sts to the left of the neckline and then knit until the armhole measures 19 (20) 21 (22) 23 (24) 25 (26) cm. Finish with a wrong-side row.

Cast off the remaining 21 (24) 26 (28) 33 (38) 43 (48) sts for the shoulder.

Right neck and shoulder as left neck, reversing shaping.

Left front

Bottom rib with garter st button band.

With 3 mm circular needle: Cast on 57 (63) 67 (73) 79 (85) 91 (97) sts.

Row 1 (WS): k5, *p2, k2*. Repeat from *–* to last 0 (2) 2 (0) 2 (0) 2 (0) sts and finish with p0 (2) 2 (0) 2 (0) 2 (0).

Row 2 (RS): Work in rib as set to last 5 sts, k5.

Row 3: k5, rib in patt as set. Repeat rows 2 and 3 until the work measures 5 cm ending with a WS row.

Continue by working in stocking stitch over the rib and 5 st garter stitch button band at the left edge (= seen from the right side) as follows: Change to 3.5 mm needles knit, and decrease 0 (1) 0 (1) 0 (0) 0 (0) sts on the first row over stocking stitch sts = 57 (62) 67 (72) 79 (85) 91 (97) sts.

Continue in stocking stitch with garter st band until the work measures 8 (9) 9 (10) 10 (10) 10 (10) cm. Finish with a wrong-side row.

Increase row: k1, M1b, knit in stocking stitch and garter stitch according to established pattern.

Repeat the increase row every 3 cm to match back shaping another 2 times = 60 (65) 70 (75) 82 (88) 94 (100) sts.

Continue in stocking stitch and garter st band until the work measures 18 (19) 20 (21) 21 (22) 22 (23) cm. Finish with a wrong-side row.

SHAPE ARMHOLE

Cast off for armhole on the right-hand side (= seen from the right side) every other row as follows: 5 (6) 6 (7) 7 (7) 7 (7) sts.

Then cast off 3 sts at beg next RS row.

Then cast off 2 sts at beg next 1 (2) 3 (3) 4 (4) 4 (4) RS rows.

Then cast off 1 st 3 (2) 3 (4) 4 (4) 4 (4) times = 47 (50) 52 (55) 60 (66) 72 (78) sts.

Cont without shaping until the armhole measures: 9 (10) 11 (12) 13 (14) 15 (16) cm ending with a WS row.

Shape neck

With RS facing, knit and place last 17 (17) 17 (18) 18 (16) 17 (18) sts on a stitch holder/scrap yarn.

Turn and cast off: 3 sts at beg next row then 2 sts at beg every other row twice, and finally one st at beg every other row twice. Work until the armhole measures 19 (20) 21 (22) 23 (24) 25 (26) cm. Finish with a wrong-side row.

Cast off the remaining 21 (24) 26 (28) 33 (41) 46 (51) sts. Mark the placement of the buttons in the garter stitch edge using safety pins. The bottom buttonhole should be 2 cm from the edge, and the top 1 cm from the neckline. The other three buttonholes are spaced evenly between these buttonholes.

Right front

Right front is made the same way as the left but mirrored. This means the garter stitch edge is placed to the right edge (= seen from the right side) and the cast off for the armhole is to the left. Start the work as follows to get the correct rib and button band placement:

Row 1 (WS): p0 (2) 2 (0) 2 (0) 2 (0) *k2, p2*. Repeat from *–* to last 5 sts, k5.

Row 2 (RS): k5, work in rib according to established pattern.

Row 3: Work in rib according to established pattern to last 5 sts, k5. N.B. Buttonholes are made (according to instructions below) in the garter stitch band to correspond with the button markers on the left front.

Buttonhole row (RS): k2, k2tog, yo, work in established pattern to end of row.

Sleeves

With 3 mm circular needle: Cast on 60 (60) 64 (64) 68 (68) 72 (72) sts.

Working back and forth:

Row 1 (WS): p1, k2 *p2, k2*. Repeat from *–* to last 1 st on the row, p1.

Row 2 (RS): k1, p2 *k2, p2*. Repeat from *–* to last 1 st on the row, k1.

Row3: p1, k2 *p2, k2*. Repeat from *–* to last 1 st on the row, p1.

Repeat rows 2 and 3 until the rib measures 5 cm ending with a WS row.

Starting a knit row, change to 3.5 mm needles and continue in stocking stitch until the work measures 12 (9) 12 (10) 15 (15) 15 (15) cm. Finish with a wrong-side row.

Increase row (RS): k1, M1b (see Techniques), knit to last 2 sts on the row, M1b, k1.

Repeat the increase row every 3 (3) 2.5 (2) 2 (2) 2 (2) cm another 9 (11) 12 (14) 15 (17) 17 (19) times = 80 (84) 90 (94) 100 (104) 108 (112) sts.

Continue in stocking stitch until the work measures 43 (44) 45 (46) 46 (47) 48 (48) cm. Finish with a wrong-side row.

Cast off as follows: 4 (4) 5 (5) 6 (6) 6 (6) sts at each end, then 3 sts at each end. Then cast off 2 sts at each end and then 1 st at each end 9 (10) 11 (12) 13 (14) 14 (14) times, then cast off 2 sts at both ends and finally 3 sts at both ends. After that, cast off the remaining 34 (36) 38 (40) 42 (44) 48 (52) sts. Make the second sleeve the same way.

Finishing

Block the cardigan carefully according to the instructions in the Knitting School, page 161. Sew the shoulder seams.

NECKBAND

With 3 mm circular needle and right side facing: Transfer the 17 (17) 17 (18) 18 (16) 17 (18) on hold from left front. Pick up 94 (94) 96 (96) 96 (104) 106 (104) sts evenly around the neckline to the sts held at right front, then transfer the 17 (17) 17 (18) 18 (16) 17 (18) sts from right front so the total number of stitches is 128 (128) 130 (132) 132 (136) 140 (140) sts. Knit 3 rows. Cast off loosely knitwise.

Sew the side seams. Then sew the sleeve seams and sew the sleeves to the armholes.

Weave in loose ends. Sew on the 5 buttons to correspond with the buttonholes.

Auntie's Cardigan

There is a photograph from my auntie Anita's childhood where she is on an outing with two other children, and in the background towers the headframe of the Stripa mine. In the picture Anita is wearing a chequered cardigan, and it piqued my interest as soon as I saw it.

I played with the simple chequered pattern and made my own version. A classic design that can either be knitted waist-length as in the picture, or normal length for those who find that more comfortable. As an extra little bonus, a blank chart and alphabet have been supplied for adding initials or a year monogram to the sleeves, if you want. You just have to draw the required letters or numbers and knit them following chart B or C.

Yarn: Järbo 2-ply ull (100% wool, 100 g = 300 m/327 yd)
Tension: 25 sts × 30 rows in stocking stitch in pattern using 3 mm (US 2.5) needles = 10 × 10 cm
Sizes: XS (S) M (L) XL (2XL) 3XL
Bust: 87 (96) 105 (115) 125 (134) 143 cm/34¼ (37¾) 41¼ (45¼) 49¼ (52¾) 56¼ in
Length: 42 (43) 45 (46) 48 (51) 53 cm/16½ (17) 17¾ (18) 19 (20) 20¾ in
Sleeve length: 48 (49) 50 (50) 50 (53) 53 cm/ 19 (19¼) 19¾ (19¾) 19¾ (20¾) 20¾ in
Amounts: Colour 1 = 300 (300) 300 (400) 450 (450) 500 g Silver Stream (no. 74104)
Colour 2 = 100 (100) 100 (150) 150 (150) (200) g Sheer Red (no. 74121)
Circular needles: 2.5 mm (US 1.5) and 3 mm (US 2.5), 80 cm
Double-pointed needles: 2.5 mm (US 1.5) and 3 mm (US 2.5)
Notions: 5 stitch markers, stitch holder, 11 buttons (10 mm in diameter), decorative band (optional), approx. 1 m
Difficulty level: 3 of 3
Construction: The cardigan is knitted in the round from the bottom up, body and sleeves are knitted separately, and then joined and knitted together at the yoke. Finally, the cardigan is cut open (see Knitting School, page 160) after the button bands are knitted on. The cardigan is decorated with a chequered pattern and on the sleeves a monogram can be included.
Adjusting the length: The cardigan in the picture is waist-length. If you want to make a 'normal' length cardigan instead, you can lengthen the body by knitting another 10 cm, or length of your choice. If you make the cardigan 10 cm longer you will need 70–100 g extra of colour 1 and 25–40 g extra of colour 2.
Techniques: M1L = increase 1 st slanting left, see Knitting School, page 163.
M1R = increase 1 st slanting right, see Knitting School, page 163.
Raglan decreases = knit to last 3 sts before raglan marker, slip 1 st, k1 and pass the slipped stitch over the knitted stich. K1, SM from left to right needle, k1, then k2tog. Repeat at all raglan stitch markers.

Body

With 2.5 mm circular needle and colour 1: Cast on 217 (241) 265 (289) 313 (337) 361 sts.

Work in rib back and forth:

Row 1 (WS): *p1, k1*, repeat from *–* to last 1 st, p1.
Row 2 (RS): *k1, p1*, repeat from *–* to last 1 st, k1.
Row 3 (WS): *p1, k1*, repeat from *–* to last 1 st, p1.

Repeat rows 2 and 3 until the rib measures 5 cm. N.B. Finish the rib with a WS row.

First row: With 3 mm circular needle – knit to end of row, then, cast on 5 steek stitches using the double twisted loop technique (see video links in the Knitting School, page 164). The steek stitches also work as a marker for the beginning and end of a rnd. (N.B. The steek stitches don't count towards the cardigan's total stitch count, and any increases or decreases should not be made within these stitches.)

From now the body is knitted in the round in stocking stitch (= knit all rows when knitting in the round).

Work the colour pattern according to chart A, reading from right to left, rows 1–6 (stitches 1–6 are repeated to last 1 st on the rnd, then knit stitch 1 in the chart). Repeat rnds 1–6 until the work measures 26 (26) 27 (28) 30 (32) 34 cm or length of your choice. N.B. Finish with rnd 1 or 4 in the chart.

Divide for body and sleeves.

Cast off as follows: Knit 50 (55) 60 (65) 70 (75) 80 sts (= right front), cast off 9 (11) 13 (15) 17 (19) 21 st (= underarm)(after casting off 1 st remain on the right needle). K98 (108) 118 (128) 138 (148) 158 sts (= back), cast off 9 (11) 13 (15) 17 (19) 21 st (= underarm)(after casting off 1 st remain on the right needle), k49 (54) 59 (64) 69 (74) 79 sts (= left front = 198 (218) 238 (258) 278 (298) 318 sts).

Place the body's stitches on a stitch holder/scrap yarn and set the work aside.

Right sleeve

With 2.5 mm dpns and colour 1: Cast on 60 (60) 60 (60) 66 (66) 66 sts.

Work in the round in rib (k1, p1) for 5 cm.

Change to 3 mm dpns, knit 1 rnd and at the same time increase 0 (0) 0 (0) 6 (6) 6 sts evenly spaced across the row = 60 (60) 60 (60) 72 (72) 72 sts.

Work the colour pattern according to chart A, rows 1–6 (stitches 1–6 are repeated to end of row). N.B. Place a stitch marker on the needle at the start of the rnd (see Knitting School, page 163) – this will make it easier to check that the pattern is knitted correctly. N.B. If monogram or year are included, these are knitted in at the middle of the sleeve starting the following row (= row 7 in the chart section). Chart B is placed over 22–40 (22–40) 22–40 (22–40) 28–46 (28–46) 28–46. Otherwise, knit according to established chequered pattern.

Repeat chart A, rows 1–6, another 1 time, and at the same time start knitting Chart B if desired.

Now, start making increases at the same time as the pattern is continued as and when new stitches are added through the increases, these should be incorporated in the established chequered pattern. N.B. The chart won't be evenly divisible across all rows. It's therefore important to keep the stitch marker in place as the starting point and let the pattern grow out to the sides.

Increase rnd: k1, M1L (see Techniques), Knit to last 1 st on the rnd, M1R (see Techniques), k1. Continue working the pattern in

stocking stitch and repeat the increase rnd every 2.5 (2.5) 2.5 (2) 2 (2) 2 cm, until 82 (86) 90 (96) 100 (106) 110 sts remain on the needle. Knit until the sleeve measures 48 (49) 50 (50) 50 (53) 53 cm, but adjust the length according to the pattern.

N.B. Finish with row 6 or 3 in the chart so that the following row is the same end row as you did for the body (= row 1 or row 4 in the chart).

Finally, cast off at the centre underarm of the sleeve, as follows: Cast off 4 (5) 6 (7) 8 (9) 10 sts, knit to last 5 (6) 7 (8) 9 (10) 11 st on the rnd, cast off 5 (6) 7 (8) 9 (10) 11 sts = 73 (75) 77 (81) 83 (87) 89 sts. Place the sleeve stitches on a stitch holder/scrap yarn and set the work aside.

Left sleeve

Is made as the right sleeve, but the pattern charts are mirrored to make the sleeves look the same seen from the front. If you wish to add in a monogram, it is placed over the following stitches: 21–39 (21–39) 21–39 (21–39) 27–45 (27–45) 27–45.

Yoke

Now all pieces are knitted together in established chequered pattern. N.B. The 4 sts before and after the raglan stitch marker are from now on knitted with colour 1.

With 3 mm circular needle and right side facing, knit the pieces together on the circular needle according to instructions on page 156. N.B. At the same time, place the stitch markers as follows: 1 marker at the start of the rnd. 1 raglan marker in the transition between right front and right sleeve, 1 raglan marker in the transition between right sleeve and the back, 1 raglan marker in the transition between the back and left sleeve and 1 raglan marker in the transition between left sleeve and left front.

You will now have these sts:

Right front: 50 (55) 60 (65) 70 (75) 80 sts.

Right sleeve: 73 (75) 77 (81) 83 (87) 89 sts.

Back: 99 (109) 119 (129) 139 (149) 159.

Left sleeve: 73 (75) 77 (81) 83 (87) 89 sts.

Left front: 50 (55) 60 (65) 70 (75) 80 sts.

Now you should have 345 (369) 393 (421) 445 (473) 497 sts on the needle.

Continue working the pattern according to chart A, with the same placement as before for each piece respectively. Let the chequered stitches on the various pieces gradually phase out as the number of stitches are decreased through the raglan decreases. This is done by always knitting the 4 sts before and after a stitch marker with colour 1 across all rows. (See note on Colourwork in the Knitting School, page 162.)

Make raglan decreases: Knit in stocking stitch and make raglan decreases (see Techniques) on every row a total of 7 (8) 8 (9) 10 (12) 14 times. Then make raglan decreases every other row a total of 19 (21) 23 (24) 25 (23) 23 times = 137 (137) 145 (157) 165 (193) 201 sts.

NECK SHAPING

Knit to last 10 (10) 10 (11) 11 (12) 12 sts before the steek stitches and then cast off 20 (20) 20 (22) 22 (24) 24 sts as well as the 5 steek stitches in the middle – to shape the neckline.

Continue knitting the row that was started with the cast off and make raglan decreases as before on this row. From now on the rest of the cardigan is knitted back and forth – continuing with the chequered pattern.

AT THE SAME TIME: Shape neck.

Turn and p2tog, then purl to end of row. Continue in stocking stitch (= knit on right side and purl on wrong side, when knitting back and forth). At the same time, decrease 1 st at the beginning of all rows, as follows: on the right side – slip 1 st, k1 st and pass the slipped stitch over the knitted stitch. On the wrong side: p2tog.

On the right side, continue with raglan decreases, until a total of 24 (26) 28 (29) 30 (30) 31 decreases have been made on every other row. (The 7 (8) 8 (9) 10 (12) 14 introductory raglan decreases are not included in this number.) N.B. The two last decrease rows are not worked in pattern but only with colour 1. After the final row with raglan decreases, work one final wrong-side row as follows: p2tog, purl to last 2 sts on the needle, p2tog = 67 (67) 75 (85) 93 (99) 97 sts.

Put these stitches on hold.

Button bands

RIGHT BUTTON BAND (WITH BUTTONHOLES)

Using 3 mm needle and colour 1 (RS): Pick up 116 (116) 118 (120) 124 (128) 132 sts along the right front edge starting from the bottom. N.B. Distribute the stitches evenly by skipping every 4th row when picking up the stitches. (= *pick up 3 sts, skip the 4th st*, repeat from *–*.)

Knit 3 rows.

Now start making the buttonholes:

(XS): k2, * k2tog, yo, k9*. Repeat from *–* another 9 times, k2tog, yo, k2.

(S): k2, *k2tog, yo, k9*. Repeat from *–* another 9 times, k2tog, yo, k2.

(M): k3, *k2tog, yo, k9*. Repeat from *–* another 9 times, k2tog, yo, k3.

(L): k4, *k2tog, yo, k9*. Repeat from *–* another 9 times, k2tog, yo, k4.

(XL): k6, *k2tog, yo, k9*. Repeat from *–* another 9 times, k2tog, yo, k6.

(2XL): k3, *k2tog, yo, k10*. Repeat from *–* another 9 times, k2tog, yo, k3.

(3XL): k5, *k2tog, yo, k10*. Repeat from *–* another 9 times, k2tog, yo, k5.

Knit 3 rows.

To make a sturdy edge that doesn't stretch with use, every 4th stitch is decreased when casting off, as follows: *Cast off 3 sts, k2tog, cast off the stitch that was knitted together*. Repeat from *–* until all stitches have been cast off. (N.B. The cast off can be finished at any stage in the repeating sequence.)

LEFT BUTTON BAND

With 3 mm needle and colour 1 (RS): Pick up 116 (116) 118 (120) 124 (128) 132 sts along the left front edge starting from the top. Knit 7 rows.

Cast off as for right button band.

Neckband

With right side facing and starting at the right button band, 3 mm needle and colour 1: Pick up new stitches along the right neckline thus – *1 st in each of the following 3 sts, skip 1 st* and repeat between *–* until you reach the stitches held for Back Neck. Knit these 67 (67) 75 (85) 93 (99) 97 sts and then pick up the same number of stitches along the left neckline as you picked up along the right neck.

Knit 5 rows, back and forth. Cast off as for right button band.

Cutting the steek

See Knitting School, page 160. Sew a reinforcing seam with sewing thread (by hand using backstitch) on each side of the middle steek stitch. Carefully cut the cardigan open in the middle of the middle steek stitch. (The cut edges will roll in towards the wrong side.)

Finishing

Sew any underarm holes together using kitchener stitch. Weave in loose ends. Block the cardigan carefully according to the instructions in the Knitting School, page 161. Sew in buttons to correspond with the buttonholes. Either cover the cut edges on the inside with a decorative band, or fold them in and sew with discreet stitches to the wrong side (see Knitting School, pages 160-161).

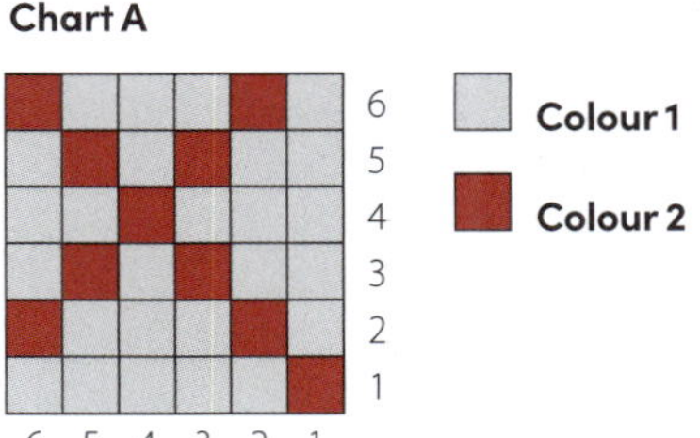

Chart B

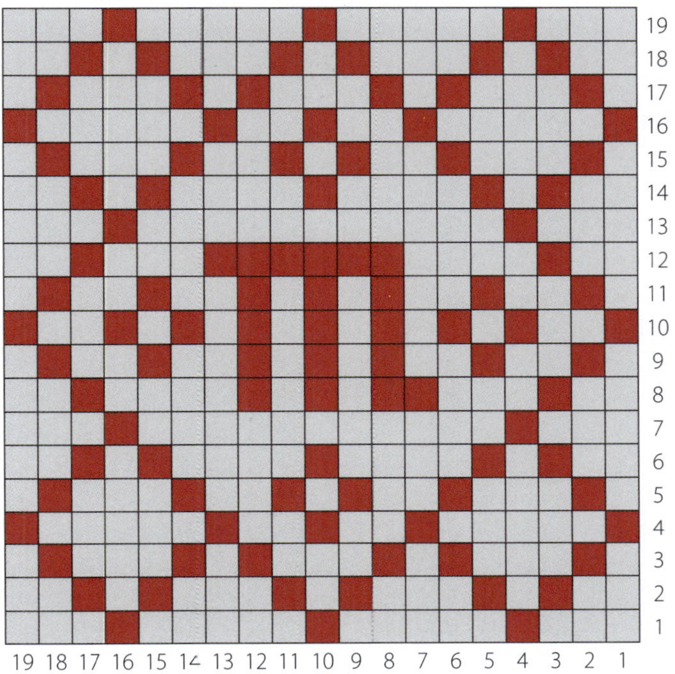

Chart C

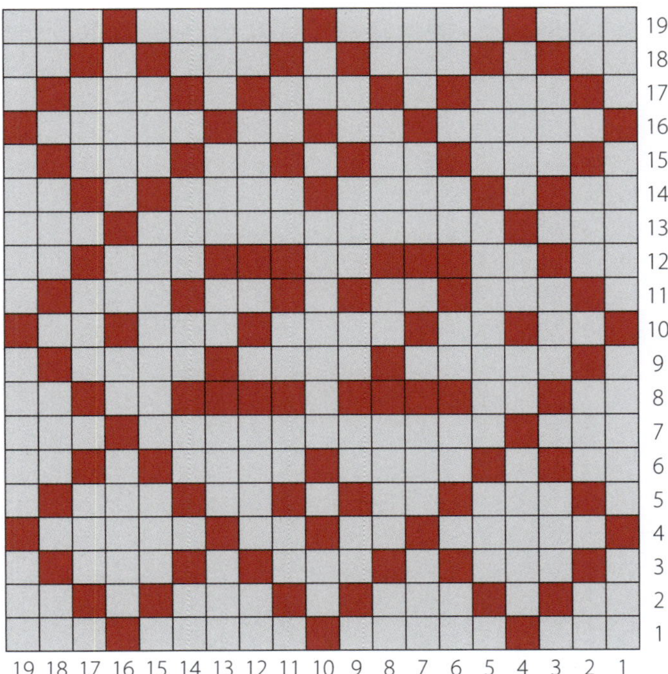

Knitting School

About knitting cardigans

The cardigans in this book

This book features cardigans with the following constructions:
1. Cardigan knitted in the round with yoke, knitted from the top and down.
Patterns: Midsummer (page 48) and Jewellery (page 134).
2. Cardigan knitted in the round with yoke, knitted from the bottom and up.
Patterns: Mirage (page 36), Wreath (page 122), Leora (page 110), Martall (page 78) and Sundborn (page 86).
3. Cardigan knitted in the round with raglan sleeves, knitted from the bottom and up. Patterns: Christmas in Bergslagen (page 128), Auntie's Cardigan (page 152), and Sisterhood (page 104).
4. Cardigan knitted in panels with sewn on sleeves.
Pattern: Silhouette (page 146).
5. Seamless cardigan with knitted on sleeves.
Patterns: Prima (page 24) and Reed (page 30).
6. Seamless cardigan with raglan sleeves, knitted from the top and down.
Patterns: Dahlia (page 54), Skathi (page 140), Fleur-de-lis (page 66), Spring Laundry (page 18) and Novel (page 92).
7. Cardigan knitted in the round with sewn-on sleeves, knitted from the bottom and up. Pattern: Legacy (page 98).
8. Seamless vest, knitted from the bottom and up.
Pattern: Hortensia (page 60).

Choosing size and calculating positive ease

The positive ease of a garment means how spacious it is, that is, how it will fit. When you choose a size, you first need to think about what fit you would prefer and then add a number of centimetres to your bust measurements.

Here's how you can calculate:

- Tight fit = add 0–5 cm/0–2 in positive ease
- Normal fit = add 5–15 cm/2–6 in positive ease
- Oversize fit = add 20–40 cm/8–16 in positive ease

This means that if you want a cardigan with a normal fit, and for example you measure 100 cm/39½ in around your bust – you should knit a cardigan that has a bust measurement of around 110 cm/43½ in. This will give you a positive ease of 10 cm/4 in. Therefore, you should choose the size that is closest to 110 cm/43½ in.

Note that most of the patterns in this book are constructed with a normal fit in mind. If a garment is designed to be tight or oversize, the pattern will make this clear.

Knitting a cardigan in the round

In the Nordic countries cardigans have traditionally been knitted in the round to make colourwork easier, since stocking stitch is only made up of knit stitches when knitting in the round. This way you don't need to knit colourwork with purl stitches, which is more time consuming. When a cardigan is knitted in the round it is cut open afterwards, to make an opening. The cut is made in the middle of a number of 'steek stitches' which are cast on in addition to the original number of stitches. This section is called the 'steek'. You could say that the steek forms a 'bridge' between the front pieces.

Techniques for cutting the steek are described in this chapter. What can be reassuring to know is that the stitches hold together very well, thanks to the wool fibres' ability to hook onto each other. Because of this there is no risk that your knitting will unravel when cutting – as long as you follow the instructions below. But keep in mind that more slippery yarns, such as cotton and acrylics, don't have the same ability to hold together, in case you choose different yarns than those that have been specified in this book.

Sewing reinforcing seams

I always sew my reinforcing seams by hand using backstitch, standard sewing thread and a sewing needle. This way I keep in control over the knitted material and can therefore avoid pulling or puckering the structure. In sewing by hand, I get a flexible and correctly placed seam in an easy and practical way. Sew one reinforcing seam on each side of the middle stitch, two reinforcing seams altogether.

Cutting the steek

When the reinforcing seams are in place it's time to cut the cardigan open. Place the cardigan on a level surface where you have a lot of room for manoeuvre.

Use a sharp and small pair of craft scissors when cutting.

Work slowly and methodically when you cut so that you are in control of what you're doing.

Let the left hand (or the right hand if you are left-handed) follow and support where you cut, so that you always make sure that the front panels are separated from the back panel. Then you don't run the risk of cutting into the back panel by mistake.

Cut the steek open by following the line in the middle of the middle stitch.

Tip: if you want to separate the front panels and the back panel completely when you cut you can pull the cardigan over an ironing board. (Pull it over with the bottom part first, so that the bottom hem ends up around the middle of the ironing board and the neckline towards the end where the ironing board narrows.) This way you will get a level surface to work on.

Mounting the cut edges

The cut edges that have rolled towards the inside once the steek has been cut, can be sewn down against the inside with yarn, darning needle and small, discreet whip stitches. Or you can cover the cut edges (band edges) by sewing on a decorative band.

Covering the cut edges with a band

Covering the cut edges on a cardigan with a decorative band is a nice finish that adds extra strength to the front edges. You need 1–2 m of band depending on the length of the cardigan, and I recommend that you choose a band that is at least 1.5 cm wide.

I like to work with bands made from materials such as cotton, wool or linen. You can of course use bands made from synthetic materials as well, but it's good if they're not too slippery on the surface, as there's a risk it will slide away while you're sewing. A band with a more matt/coarser surface will lie in place and bond with the knitted structure, which makes the sewing easier. It's nice to use interwoven bands, that is bands where the pattern is woven instead of printed. These bands are very durable. But there are plenty of printed bands with both pretty and fun designs, these also work very well. Finally, always choose bands of good quality so that the design doesn't risk fading in the wash.

If you are making band edges on your cardigan, it's important that both edges remain the same length, meaning that none of the edges is stretched out more than the other when the band is sewn on. Therefore, the band should be cut into two equal lengths before you do anything else. Measure the length on one of the cut edges when stretched out to a good length. Then add 2 cm seam allowance at each end (total 4 cm).

Pin both bands to the inside of the cardigan so that they cover the cut edges and fold in the edges at each end. Make sure the cut edges are stretched evenly underneath the bands. Then sew the edges of the bands in place with sewing thread using small and discreet stitches.

Knitting two sleeves at the same time

By using two sets of dpns or two short circular needles – alternatively one long circular needle (80 cm) and the *magic loop* technique – you can knit both sleeves simultaneously. You then knit one section at the time on each sleeve, or each row at the same time if you choose the *magic loop* alternative. (Search YouTube for videos explaining the *magic loop* technique.)

This way it's easy to get increases, decreases and possible adjustment the same on both sleeves, while you have them fresh in your memory. In addition, there is no chance that sleeve number two remains unknitted, since both sleeves grow simultaneously.

The cardigan is carefully cut open right in the middle of the middle stitch. It's a good idea to hold your free hand as support and protection to avoid cutting into the back panel.

Avoiding holes underneath the sleeves

When you knit on sleeves and come to the transition between the new stitches and the stitches that have been put on hold from the yoke, there is a risk that a hole appears at the place of the transition. I usually solve it by picking up a stitch in one of the loops right at the point of the transition and placing it on the left needle, and then knit it together with the first of the stitches that was put on hold.

Then knit the rest of the on-hold stitches. Avoid a hole at the next transition by picking up a stitch in one of the loops at the transition, as well as an ordinary stitch of the ones that are being picked up. Place these two stitches on the left needle and knit them together. Then continue picking up the remaining new stitches.

Finishing

Blocking a cardigan

1. Fill a sink, tub or bucket with tepid water.
2. Add a dash of wool detergent. (There are various brands on the market, with or without fragrance, and most of them have a slightly softening quality.)
3. Soak the cardigan carefully. Don't rub or stretch, just let the water soak through the garment gradually by turning and moving the garment around in the water.
4. Then rinse the cardigan 2–3 times in water without anything added. In this step the water should also be tepid, that is, the same temperature as before.

Drying and shaping

1. Take the cardigan out of the water and spread it out on a dry and clean terry towel. Squeeze out the water by rolling up the towel and cardigan to a hard roll. Place the roll on the floor and step on it to squeeze out as much water as possible.
2. Spread the cardigan out on a level, clean and dry surface – for example a dry terry towel, a rug or a blocking mat.
3. Shape the cardigan so that it is lying flat without any folds or creases, and so that the proportions look good. This step is easiest if you have a blocking mat, since the coarse surface means it's easy to get the cardigan to stay in its required place. On a blocking mat you can also pin specific parts in their right position, by using special stainless steel blocking pins. You should avoid stretching the garment too much, but if necessary you can carefully try to widen or lengthen parts of a cardigan that have ended up with slightly wrong proportions – for example a button edge that is slightly shorter than the actual cardigan, or a sleeve that seems narrower than the other sleeve. It's good to take your time on this step so that you shape the garment carefully with your hands, making it as straight and smooth as possible.
4. Then let the cardigan dry flat, preferably in a warm place, until completely dry. Repeat this procedure when your cardigan needs washing again.

Choosing buttons

Buttons are an important and beautiful detail on your cardigan. The book features buttons of many different materials: mother of pearl, wood, leather, porcelain, metal and plastic.

I prefer buttons made from a natural material, such as wood or mother of pearl (particularly antique ones of good quality). These materials go so well together with wool and age beautifully from use. At the same time it can be fun to use plastic, glass or porcelain if you want to match a specific colour in the cardigan's pattern.

Sewing on buttons

I always sew on buttons using double sewing thread. This is what my friend Kerstin taught me making it twice as fast.

Method: Thread the needle, pull the thread through so that the needle ends up at the middle of the thread's length. Tie a knot at the end and then sew the button on.

Mending a worn-down cardigan

If your cardigan has become worn-down at the elbows you can reinforce the structure with help of kitchener stitch. In this video I show you how: www.bit.ly/3tsrPFS

Mending rib cuffs on a cardigan

If the cuffs of your cardigan get worn down and tear at the ends, you can knit on new cuffs.

Method: Divide/place the stitches of the cuff onto four dpns by threading on every other loop onto the needles. This is done at a point where the structure is still intact. Cut off the worn-down section but leave around 1 cm of knitted rib next to the needles.

Using the same or a similar yarn to what's been used for the cardigan, knit new rib to length of your choice. Cast off in rib.

Unravel the remaining part of the old cuff and weave in loose ends on the inside.

Futureproofing your cardigan

It's nice to add an extra button to the inside of the cardigan, so that it's there as a spare in case one of the cardigan's buttons drops off and gets lost. You can also wind some 'darning yarn' onto one of the leftover yarn ball bands, and keep this in a folder. This makes it easy to find the right yarn when the cardigan needs mending, increasing the longevity of your garment.

Techniques featured in the book

Colourwork

Knitting patterns using two or several colours at the same time is a common technique in Swedish and Nordic knitting traditions. The technique gives a dense and warming structure since you end up with double or triple strands of yarn as you knit.

There are different ways of holding the yarn when you knit colourwork. In Sweden it's common to hold the yarn in your left hand: one thread over the index finger and one over the middle finger, then you gather the threads in the hand and hold them together with your ring finger and little finger. But there are other ways of holding the yarn – I hold one thread over my thumb and one over my index finger, for example. Try and see what works the best for you! The most important thing is that you can keep an even tension in both threads, so that the yarn that is on hold for the moment doesn't pull at the backside.

When you knit a pattern using two colours, you usually regard one colour as the dominant colour (the highlight) and the other as the background. You should hold the yarn so that the dominant colour sits closest to the work and the yarn is always carried under. This way these stitches will become dominant and be more visible than the background. The background colour should instead sit furthest away from the work and always be carried over. It's important to be consistent with the order of the colours, otherwise the pattern will become unclear.

When knitting with one colour, the other will run along at the back. The thread at the back should have the same tension as the rest of the work, otherwise the knitting will get bumpy (if you pull it too tight) or shapeless (if you don't pull it enough).

If you knit more than 3–4 consecutive stitches in the same colour it can be a good idea to catch the yarn that runs along the back by wrapping the yarn you're knitting with around it. This way you avoid long 'floats', threads that catch easily when you put on or take off a garment. Just make sure not to catch the yarn at the same place on several consecutive rounds; instead change the placement for each round – otherwise the thread at the back can become visible through the knitting.

To get a successful end result when knitting colourwork, it's important that you:

- Keep your tension as even as possible.
- Keep a good tension on the thread that runs at the back.
- Hold the pattern colour and the background colour in the same order every round.
- Catch the yarn when knitting more than 3–4 consecutive stitches in the same colour.
- Don't catch the yarn at the same place on several consecutive rounds.

Shaping a raised section on the back panel

For several of the seamless cardigans in this book, a raised section is knitted in the middle of the back using short rows. The back panel will then become a little higher than the front, which makes the cardigan sit comfortably around the neck and gives a better fit.

Short rows

Short rows means they are worked by turning before you have knitted the whole row, meaning you only knit a part of a row. To prevent a hole from forming where you turn, the stitches are wrapped (see below) when turning. This technique is used to form a raised section at the back panel of many cardigans in this book.

Wrap and turn

ON THE RIGHT SIDE: Place the thread at the front of the work, slip next stitch moving it to the right needle. Place the thread at the back of the work and then move the slipped stitch back to the left needle. Turn. The thread is now wrapped around the stitch.
ON THE WRONG SIDE: Place the thread at the back of the work, slip the next stitch moving it to the right needle. Place the thread at the front of the work and move the stitch back to the left needle. Turn. The thread is now wrapped around the stitch.
WORKING A WRAPPED STITCH: When you work a wrapped stitch you go through both the stitch itself and the wrapped thread at the same time – knit on the right side and purl on the wrong side.

Place and slip marker

Stitch markers are practical little tools made from plastic or metal, for example, that are placed on the needle between two stitches. In the book, stitch markers are used regularly to mark where the raglan sleeves are placed. 'Slip marker' means that you slip the marker from the left needle to the right. N.B. You can easily make your own stitch markers from tied yarn ends.

Abbreviations

k = knit stitch
k1tbl = twisted knit stitch. Knit the stitch through the back loop
p1tbl = twisted purl stitch. Purl the stitch through the back loop.
SL1pw = slip one stitch purlwise
wyif = with yarn in front
l = loop
M1L = increase 1 st slanting left
M1R = increase 1 st slanting right
M1PR = pick up the thread between 2 sts from the back with the left needle and purl through the front loop
M1PL = pick up the thread between 2 sts from the front with the left needle and purl through the back loop
p = purl
PM = place marker
RS = right side
beg = beginning
SM = slip marker
st/s = stitch/es
tog = together
WS = wrong side
RS = right side
yo = yarn over
dpns = double-pointed needles
rnd = round
dec = decrease
M1b = increase 1 st in the stitch below

Decreases

DECREASE SLANTING RIGHT: Knit 2 stitches together (k2tog) = 1 stitch decreased.
DECREASE SLANTING LEFT: Slip 1 stitch, knit 1 and pass the slipped stitch over the knitted stitch = 1 stitch decreased.

Increases, three variations

INCREASE SLANTING LEFT (M1L)

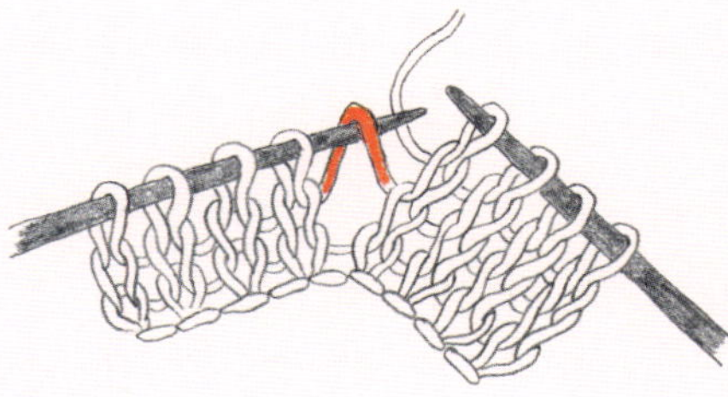

1. Pick up the thread in between the stitches, from the front with the left needle, to form a new stitch.

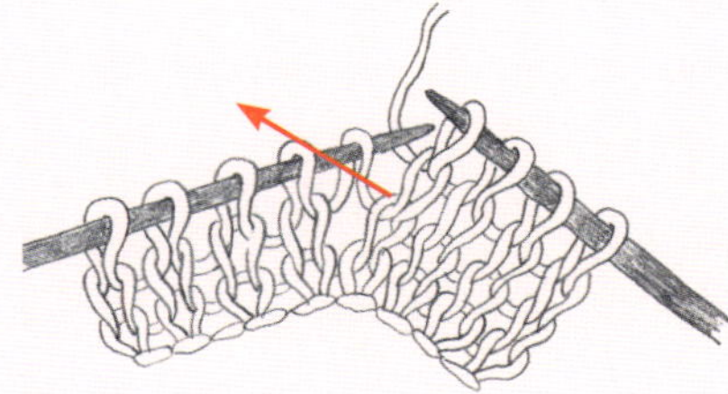

2. Knit 1 stitch through the back loop, as the arrow shows.

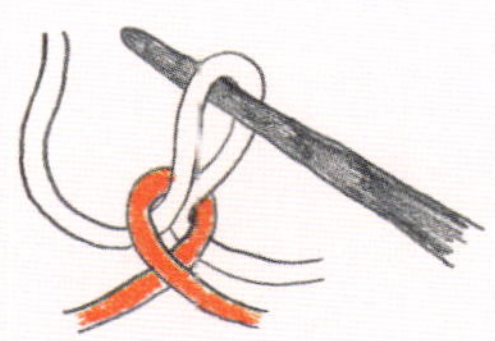

3. A new stitch slanting left has been made.

INCREASE SLANTING RIGHT (M1R)

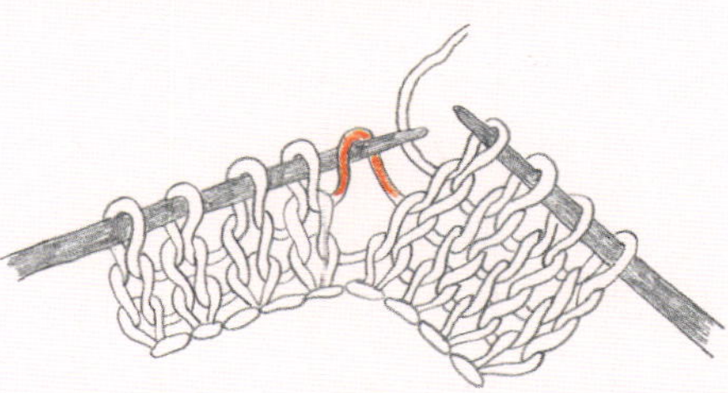

1. Pick up the thread in between the stitches, from behind with left needle, to form a new stitch.

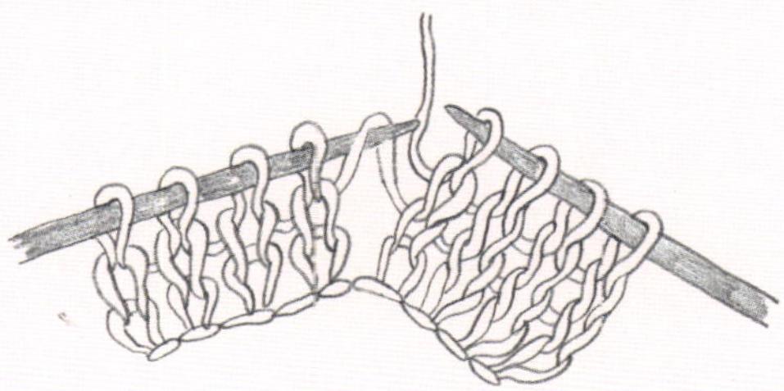

2. Knit 1 through the front loop, as the arrow shows.

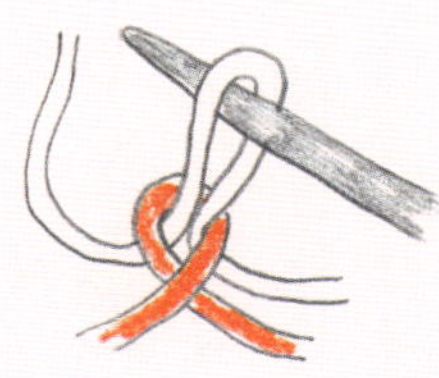

3. A new stitch slanting right has been made.

INVISIBLE INCREASE IN THE STITCH BELOW (M1B)

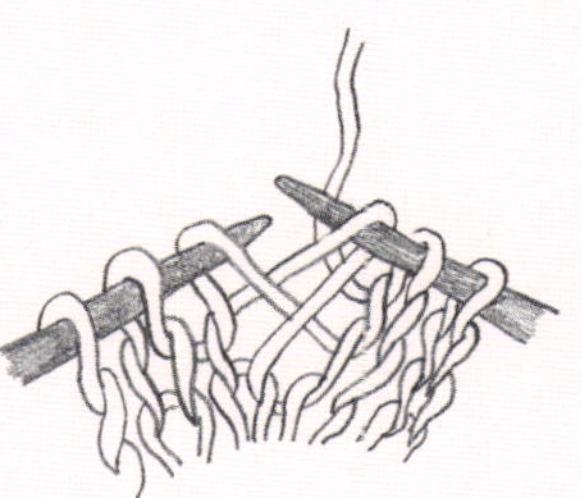

1. Insert the right needle into the stitch below the next stitch on the LHS. Pick up the stitch and place on the left needle.

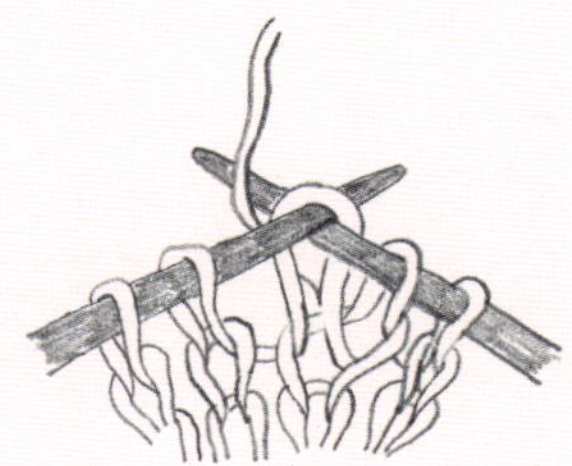

2. Knit 1 through the front loop of the new stitch, and then knit 1 in the original stitch.

Latvian braid

Row 1: *k1 with colour 1, k1 with colour 2*. Repeat from *–* to end of row.

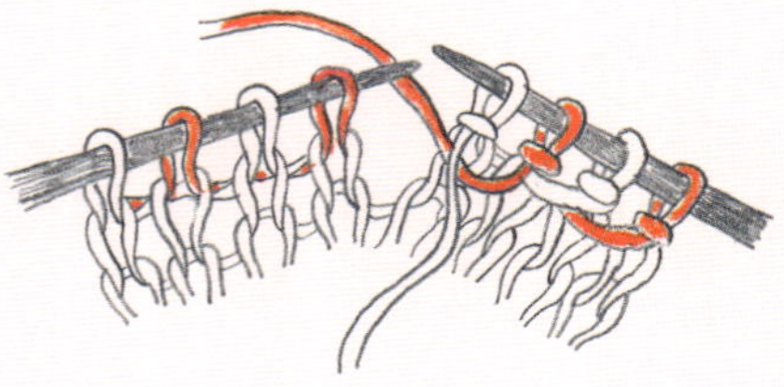

Row 2: *p1 with colour 1, p1 with colour 2*. Repeat from *–* to end of row. N.B. Hold both threads at the front of the work when you knit. For every colour change, the new yarn should be passed underneath the yarn that you have just knitted with.

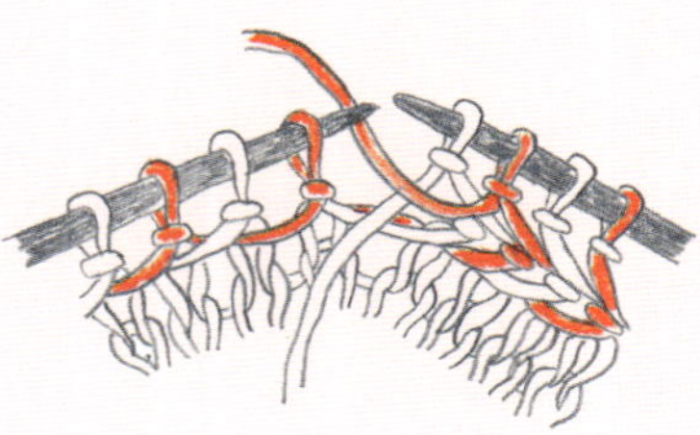

Row 3: *p1 with colour 1, p1 with colour 2*. Repeat from *–* To end of row. N.B. Hold both threads at the front of the work when you knit. For every colour change, the new yarn should be passed underneath the yarn that you have just knitted with.

Joining with kitchener stitch

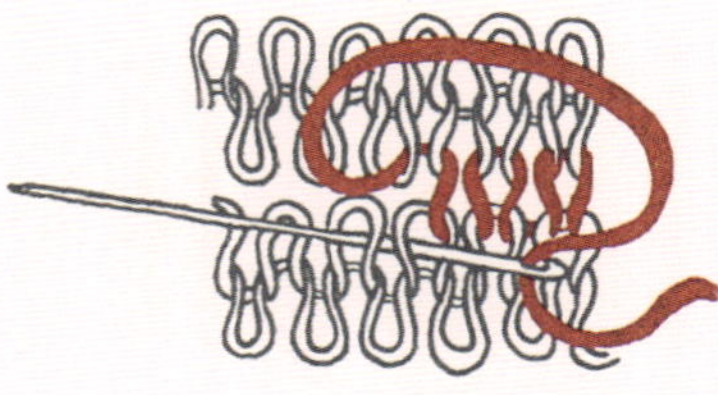

When you sew two parts together using kitchener stitch you get an invisible seam. The stitches disappear into the knitted structure without any bulky seams appearing.

3-needle cast off

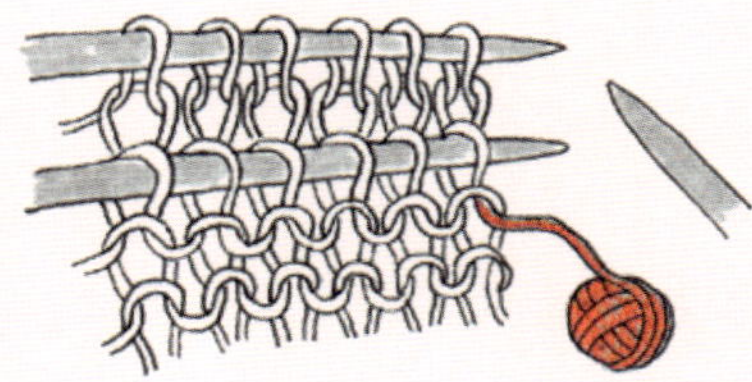

1. Cut the yarn, but leave a length to cast off with. Divide the stitches over 2 needles. Place the right sides facing each other so that the wrong sides are facing outwards. Place the needles parallel to each other.

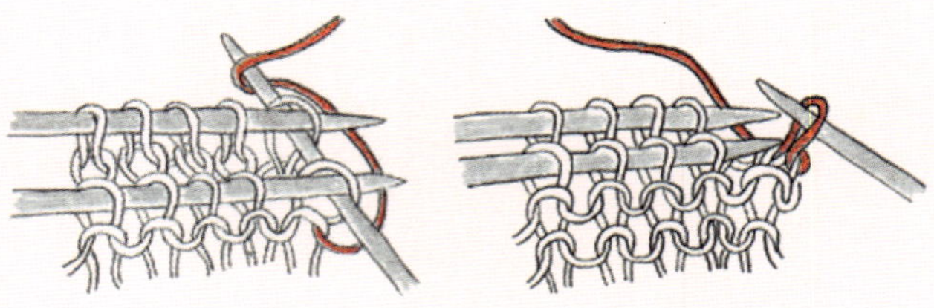

2–3. K1 through 2 sts (= 1 st from each needle).

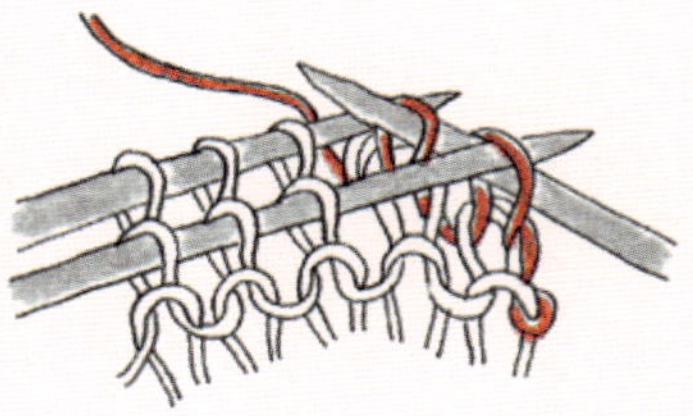

4. K1 through 2 sts.

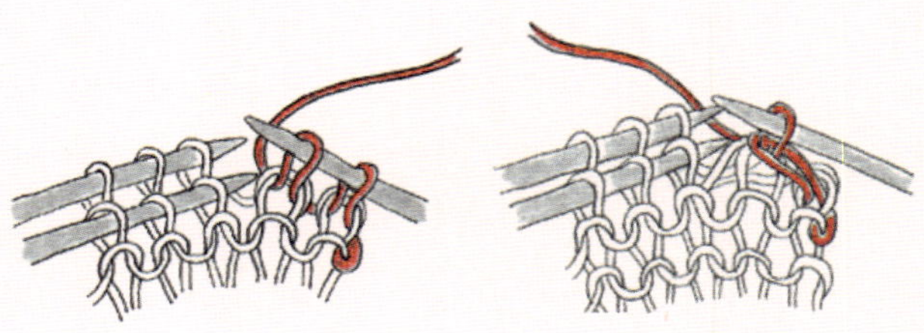

5–6. Pass the stitch that you knitted first over the second stitch. Repeat the steps on pictures 4–6 until all stitches have been cast off.

Video links

Here we have gathered together links for instructional videos that clearly show certain technical methods in the book.

Double twisted loop technique = *www.bit.ly/3xjjdCs*
Italian cast on = *www.bit.ly/3O8ywVg*
Italian cast off = *www.bit.ly/3zz3rGj*

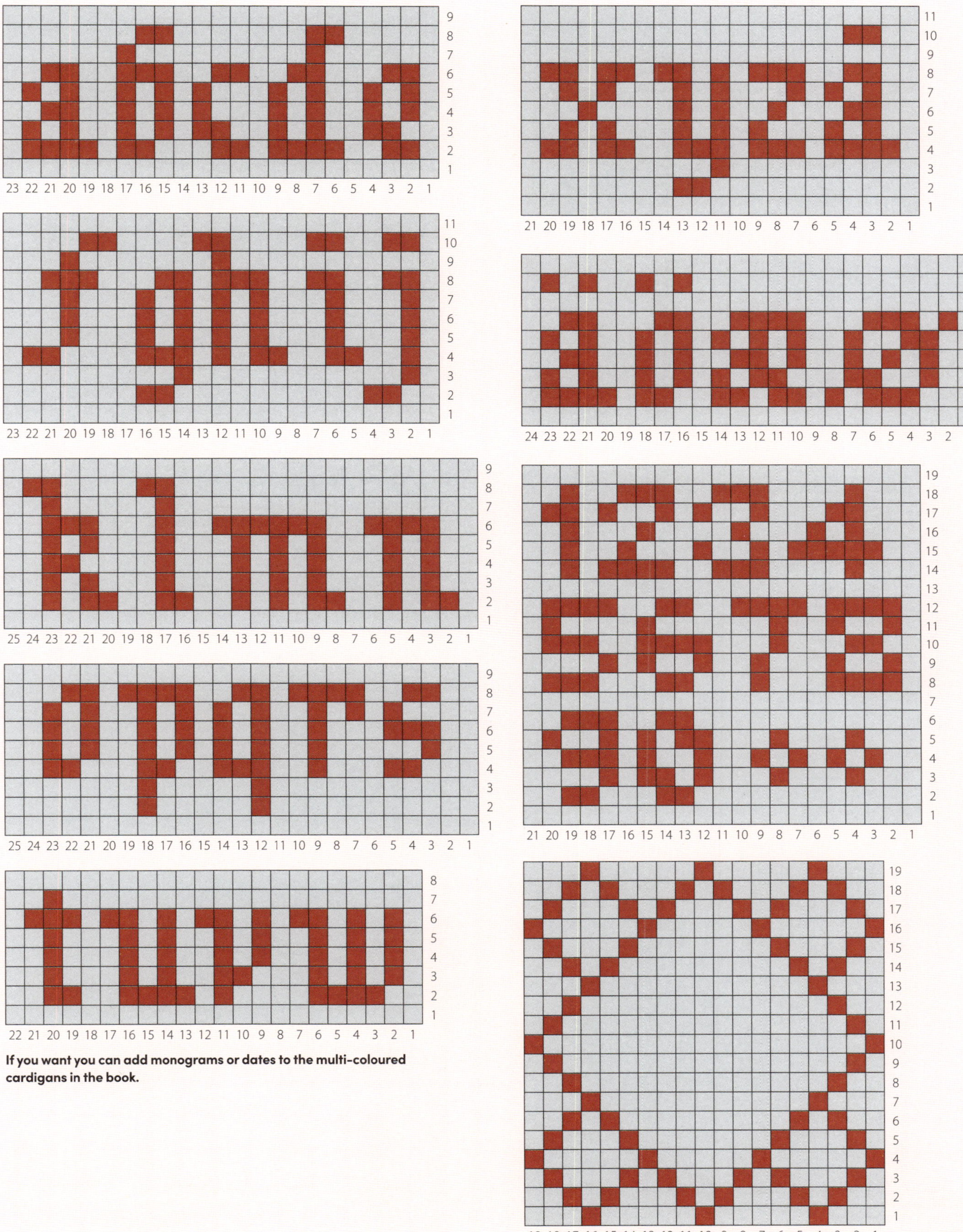

If you want you can add monograms or dates to the multi-coloured cardigans in the book.

Blank chart for Auntie's Cardigan on page 152. Here you can fill in initial or year. You could, for example, have the year on one arm and an initial on the other.

Index

Yarns used in the book

Järbo

Järbo is a Swedish yarn company with textile traditions going back to the 1800s.
www.jarbo.se

Fin Mohair Silke
72% mohair, 28% silk
25 g = 210 m/229 yd

Järbo 2-ply wool
100% pure new wool
100 g = 300 m/327 yd

Llama Silk
70% soft baby llama, 30% mulberry silk
50 g = 165 m/180 yd

Select no. 1 (Mohair Tweed Yarn from Donegal)
70% merino, 30% mohair
50 g = 110 m/120 yd

Svensk Ull 3-ply
100% Swedish wool
100 g = 180 m/196 yd

Llama Soft from Järbo
85% soft baby llama, 15% polyamide
50 g = 150 m/164 yd

Ístex

Ístex is an Icelandic yarn company whose production of domestic wool yarn has its roots in the 1800s.
www.istex.is

Léttlopi
100% Icelandic wool
50 g = 100 m/109 yd

Plötulopi
100% Icelandic wool
100 g = 300 m/327 yd

Rauma Garn

Rauma Ullvarefabrikk produces traditional wool yarn from Norwegian wool. The company has been operating since 1927.
www.raumaull.no

Rauma Finull
100% pure new wool
50 g = 175 m/191 yd

Sandnes

Sandnes Garn produces yarn for hand knitting from wool and other materials. The company has been operating since 1888.
www.sandnesgarn.no

Børstet Alpakka
96% brushed alpaca, 4% Nylon
ca 50 g = 110 m/120 yd

Sandnes Sisu
80% wool, 20% nylon
approx. 50 g = 175 m/191 yd

Thank you

Helén – the best photographer! Every book is like an adventure – I really appreciate working with you.
Anna-Karin – for stylish design and clever solutions.
Annika – for always being there with your calmness and experience. It feels so safe to work with you.
Eva – for yet another fine collaboration. I'm so pleased we could make this book together and grateful for your support during the creative process.
Carol – for good advice and invaluable help with the technical editing.
Lina – for skilfulness, meticulousness and helpfulness. You rock!
Bonnier Fakta – my lovely Swedish publisher – for having faith in me.
Pernilla Olesen – for magnificent knitting help, when my time wasn't enough.
Lydias Garn – for yarn sponsorship and continuous encouragement. You mean a lot to me.
Kerstin E – for continuous support and for turning doubts into joy in such a nice way.
Kerstin C – for enjoyable knitting evenings, the best cakes and for being so caring.
Fredrika – for everything, dear friend! I look forward to celebrating the book release with you.
Monika – for nice times just the two of us. And for a shared interest in knitting.
Anita – because you are my aunt. I'm so pleased that your little cardigan got to become a big one in my book!
Lisa – for the sisterhood! It's so nice to see that you are also knitting now.
Mum and dad – for everything you do and for letting me share every step of the book publishing process with you. It makes all the difference to me.
Daniel and Greta – for love, patience and support through everything. You are my favourite people!
Family, friends and colleagues – for everyday encouragement, when its needed the most.
Knitters, readers and followers – for knitting my patterns. This book is for you!

Photo locations

Carl Larsson house in Sundborn (*www.carllarsson.se*)
Siggebohyttans miner's estate (*www.olm.se*)
The Dahlia Park in Enskede (*www.dahliaentusiasterna.se*)
Thanks to those who lent us the rowboat on Ljusterö!
Thank you Lena, for lending us the fisherman's cottage in Undal!

Models

Sophia Brännvall
Anna Karlsson
Greta Nolgård
Franka Sjöström
Zelda Sjöström
Johanna Wahlberg
My warmest thanks to you all!

Makeup & hair

Michelle Vallin – thank you for your fantastic commitment!
Angelica Nilsson – it's so nice that you helped out when we needed it the most!

For more inspiration and knitting tips – follow me on Instagram: *@majasmanufaktur*. There you can also ask questions about the cardigans in the book.

Have you knitted something from the book? Share it on social media with the hashtag #MajasCardigans.

First published in the United Kingdom
in English by
Batsford
43 Great Ormond Street
London
WC1N 3HZ

An imprint of B. T. Batsford Holdings Limited

ISBN 9781849949156

A CIP catalogue record for this book is available from the British Library.

10 9 8 7 6 5 4 3 2

Reproduction by Rival Colour Ltd, UK
Printed and bound by Dream Colour, China

This book can be ordered direct from the publisher at www.batsfordbooks.com, or try your local bookshop.

Distributed throughout the UK and Europe by Abrams & Chronicle Books, 1st Floor, 22–24 Ely Place, London EC1N 6TE and 57 rue Gaston Tessier, 75166 Paris, France

www.abramsandchronicle.co.uk
info@abramsandchronicle.co.uk